TROPICAL GHANA
KITCHEN DATE

TROPICAL GHANA KITCHEN DATE

Rediscover Your Tropical Side with Simple, Fun, Delicious and Wholesome Ghanaian Recipes

CHARLES A. CANN

First Printing

ISBN: 979-8-9897230-2-7

Design: Charles A. Cann
Editorial: Tiffany Sakato
Photography: Charles A. Cann
Additional photography: Thomas Lee, Peter Galassi, James Taylor, Munlai

For more information, please visit www.tropicalghana.com

To all who love Ghanaian cuisine, crave West African flavours and are interested in exploring tropical ingredients to enjoy finger-licking recipes with their family, friends and loved ones.

To the Tropical Ghana family and everyone who loves cooking; and tries to eat wholesome and a little better every day to expand their food choices.

To everyone who is looking to rediscover their tropical side and looking for new, simple, fun and wholesome recipes to make delicious fresh plates of food.

To anyone looking for a unique Ghanaian and West African food experience in their own kitchen or backyard.

To every kid, boy or girl, young man or young woman, ready or not, who is about to change the world; be positive, be inspired, be encouraged and be empowered to make your remarkable impact.

To all my Ghana Jollof Rice lovers and future Ghana Jollof Rice converts, the talk will continue because you are on the right team.

#TropicalGhanaKitchenDate
#RediscoverYourTropicalSide
#RediscoverYourTropicalGhanaSide

★ SPECIAL THANKS

To you Lord God, thank you for the gift of life and for your grace, for your amazing love, for the strength to move and shake things up, and for the blessing of cooking delicious food as well as showing me kindness to share the blessing with the world. Continue to guide me and lead me so I can follow as I continue to cook and share more recipes with others.

To my late grandparents, K.T. Glover and Beatrice Naa Koshie Glover, thanks for preparing this place for us and thanks for going to prepare the next place. To the late Kate Okailey Brenya, thank you very much for everything. The love, the steps, as well as discipline you showed me in the kitchen, is what continues to guide me to be disciplined and work with a smile when I touch food. To the late Felix B. Brenya, thank you for the opportunity to learn about farming and animals – how to treat and raise them well – plus everything else you added to my life.

To my mother, Rose Glover, for playing a big role in my life's journey from the very beginning to when it took a stop in Chicago – where my cooking got reignited and new building blocks got added for me to bring a little bit more spice to the world. To my family, if cooking is an infection, then it's a real good one; and I sure caught it. Keep whipping up tasty meals. I salute all of you who supported this mission and stood with me when the going got tough.

To the late Ms. Joanna Baddoo, for all the food conversations. To Hawa Salifu, for taking time to share your in-depth knowledge of ingredients, techniques and foods of Ghana. To Pat Ledi, for all your help and for believing in me. To Abdulai Mumuni, for looking out for your brother and the bits and pieces you keep adding.

To Tiffany Sakato for your wonderful work as editor and for all of your input and final touches. To Thomas Lee, thank you very much for your photos and all of your support over the years. To Cynthia Moreno, for all of your comments, feedback, and for looking out for the Tropical Ghana family. To Peter Galassi, for your keen interest, commitment and feedback to all things Tropical Ghana since day one. To Mr. Garland, for your excitement, commitment, and dedication to the Tropical Ghana cause. To Comfort Ocran, Maame Ama Afful, Joseph Asare Jnr., Anthony Amuzu, Minnie Quartey-Cofie, Valerie Titus-Glover, James F. Taylor, Delphina Oparebea Anipare, Emmanuel Nii Sackey Quarcoopome, Benjamin Tawiah, Michael Fuchs, Matt Tomko, Pedro Padilla, Osato Dixon, Brian Parrish, Shane Duckworth, Mrs. Asare-Yeboah, The Asare-Yeboahs, for your enthusiasm, help, and spreading the message far and wide.

To Linda Kolbusz-Kosan, it was like the heavens opened and you fell from it. Thanks for believing in me and for being a blessing in my life, as well as for always checking in even when I am off the radar. To Rev. Festus Johnson for all of your prayers, positive energy, jokes and looking out for me.

To the Amy, Stephen and the Court Tree Collective family, for collaborating and helping to bring fresh, exciting energy to Brooklyn, New York, as well as spice up the Brooklyn air with fresh new African flavours. To the New Yorkers that I have met who understand the hustle is real and they keep at it. To all the parents, mothers, aunties, grandmothers, fathers and families hard at work and cooking for their families in my homeland, Ghana and beyond. To everyone who gave me and continues to give me honest opinions after tasting Tropical Ghana recipes. To all who made it to one of the many cooking classes or a food event or any of the food workshops, as well as for all of the feedback you offered and the encouraging smiles on your faces after enjoying Tropical Ghana cooking.

To every person who contributed his or her time, and resources, and helped make this book possible. And to all my many, many, many friends and fans, who on countless occasions talk about my cooking and continue to show their loving support – you go, Tropical Ghana family!

Blema ni hoomor kɛ ha ŋmɛnɛŋmɛnɛ nikasemo kɛ wɔsɛ anɔkwale kɛ sɛnamɔ

Cooking from past generations for today's learning and truthful future preservation and benefits

CONTENTS

 # INTRODUCTION

What is a tropical Ghana kitchen date?

tropical Ghana kitchen date
   fun, learning, empowering and bonding activity with tropical Ghana cooking

> have a **tropical Ghana kitchen date**
   : 1.
      to spend time together with family, friends or loved ones to prepare and cook a meal together, eat as you enjoy each other's company with loads of laughter and with open arms to clean up afterwards

   - *Mansa, I want us to have a tropical Ghana kitchen date if you're around this weekend.*

   : 2.
      to cook a fresh plate of food, share the plate with someone amidst smiles, stories, maybe some singing, dancing, and definitely tidying up at the end

   - *That's what I'm talking about, Kofi! It's a tropical Ghana kitchen date! We shall meet at the market on Saturday morning to buy fresh ingredients then.*

   - *Are you still in traffic, Naa? The tropical Ghana kitchen date has started without you and we're all wondering how come you are still not here. You better have a good excuse!*

   - *I can't believe you missed the tropical Ghana kitchen date last time. Seriously?*

"Have a bite! Try a piece! Just a tiny bit! Have a slice! Taste it! Just a sip! Let's finish this piece together!" There are many ways humans invite each other to taste food or join in a meal.

During one of my food events, a lad in a gray cardigan approached me and asked what I was serving. After explaining, he ran off with a full plate without a trace. He literally vanished among the gathering! Gone; just like that! I guess that's what kids do or what some of us did when we were that young.

Moments later, someone got my attention as I was busy into service. When I found the voice, my new friend, the lad in the gray cardigan, was back with another person who looked even younger than him but with some semblance. Perhaps, siblings but one was clearly taller and older. Obviously, their mission was sourcing more edibles.

I put a fresh plate together for them. Gray Cardigan Lad put the plate to his younger brother's face. The younger brother was hesitant and out of the mouth of my first new friend landed the words, "ohh taste!" Yes, they were Ghanaian kids. And Ghanaians have a very special way of inviting each other to eat when the person offering the bite encounters some form of resistance.

"Come on, try it and stop the ruff!" A broad smile occupied his whole lower face as the plate in his hands inched closer and closer to his younger brother's face. "Just taste it! Ohh, taste la! My friend, if you don't try it and it finishes; don't blame me ohh!" Something about Ghanaians and the ways they nicely push each other into having a sample of food is unexplainable. Meanwhile, the Gray Cardigan Lad continued with his persuasion but a bit more "tactfully." " Taste it please," he calmly whispered.

When the younger brother reached into the plate and put a piece in his mouth, the latter's face lit up instantly and ended in a joyous smile. And that was the moment! It was a very precious magical food moment that played right in front of my eyes. I knew that moment was one special moment – a kitchen date! Tropical Ghana Kitchen Date begins!

Piece by Piece – The Journey to *Tropical Ghana Kitchen Date*

Most times when I meet a person who has visited Ghana and he or she learns I am a native of the land, the conversation easily drifts to Ghanaian food and its uniqueness. Often, I will hear something like, "You have no idea how delicious the soup was; I can't even describe it!" And the memorable one I cannot shake off, "Oh mine, the Red Red! I want some now. Can you make it for me, please?" It does not stop there.

Fresh-tasting food is very inviting, and its aroma appeals to any human's sense of smell. The minute food comes into physical contact with the mouth, it makes its journey by awakening all of the other senses with fresh melodies of joy and nutrients. This is simply magical! It's all about that initial taste that ignites a powerful feeling! What better way to have a taste of Ghana, a taste of West Africa, a taste of tropical ingredients, a taste of good, fresh food than to actually experience cooking, tasting and enjoying the food as it takes you on a magical journey with your loved ones.

When you taste food, sometimes it can be sweet, bitter, tangy, zesty, sour, delicious, peppery, tantalizing, tart, crisp, vinegary, zippy, hot, flavoursome, fiery, highly seasoned, aromatic, biting, crunchy, bland, dull, appetizing, savoury, crusty, stinging, spicy, sharp, kicking; or it's simply "Mmm, tasty! I want more!"

Tropical Ghana Kitchen Date is a special cookbook about coming together with loved ones and cooking fresh food that keeps more than Ghana and West Africa on your mind. It's a commitment to eat fresh, delicious food that is simple and fun to make, and wholesome for the needed nutritional boost to recharge right away and keep going.

In this special cookbook, I share some of my favourite Ghanaian recipes that I grew up on, as well as new and exciting original recipes: Highlife Salad, Cucumber On Date Salad, Sunset Salad, Aluguntugui Delight, Sobolo Mango Smoothie, Shrimp Something, 1-2-3 Ghana Pepper Chicken, Blema Turkey Kpakpa, Brown Rice Ghana Jollof Rice, New York Ginger Mint Cookies, Cocoa Plantain, and many more that will send you on a Ghanaian food plot twist. You will be venturing into cooking the recipes that have also been featured at most of my cooking classes and workshops right in your own kitchen or backyard.

It is an honour to come from the country that's closest to the middle of the Earth and share my food with you. In terms of geographical coordinates, Ghana is the closest country to Latitude 0°, the equator, while Longitude 0°, the Greenwich Meridian, passes through the country. So it feels as if I am sharing recipes from people of the centre of the Earth with everyone around the globe.

Tropical Ghana Kitchen Date is a cookbook that can help you create a unique Ghanaian and West African food experience wherever you can find tropical ingredients no matter where you find yourself in the world. It's love, goodness, and nourishment from the motherland – a really good slice of the mother continent, Africa, wherever you go.

Good Food! Good Friendship! Good Humour!

Good food, good friendship and good humor when found in one place excites, uplifts and is definitely a morale booster any day. The journey has been filled with good food, good friendships and loads of good humour.

More than 18 years ago, I was pushed by some friends to keep cooking to help them satisfy their newly discovered craving for Ghanaian food and for others to reconnect with some of their favourite Ghanaian dishes. When I was growing up in Ghana, kids referred to each other or people who were passionate food lovers or those who simply loved food as "Foodians." I met these enthusiastic friends of mine at Northwestern University in Evanston, near Chicago. I am nicknaming them from now on as "The Chicago Foodians." So, The Chicago Foodians reignited my cooking, really sparked a deeper passion, and "chased" me to cook for them regularly. But I could not keep up with their numerous requests, and neither was I able to flee nor be completely out of their reach.

At that time, I planned to create an online cooking resource for The Chicago Foodians so they could refer to it for recipes. I convinced myself that it would end as a win-win for both parties and we can all call it a lovely day afterwards. That did not happen as planned! The Chicago Foodians kept requesting for more recipes even after I had left Chicago for New York City. There was no end in sight as I had originally envisioned. Clearly, my "getaway" to a new city did not even come close to ending the chapter. Rather, the heavens opened! I was blessed with an idea.

In 2006, the Tropical Ghana Cookbook Project came to life in Harlem, New York City. In 2007, I had the opportunity to publish my first cookbook, *Tropical Ghana Delights*. Yet again, the plan was to get The Chicago Foodians a book to help them satisfy their newfound love for Ghanaian cooking, help others reconnect and pretty much end the story there. Little did I know it was the beginning of something new; something I had never ever thought of, not even in my wildest imagination or even considered in all my plans. I am most grateful to God for showing me love and kindness as well as for the blessing and talent to share my cooking, and the time and energy with others in order for more and more people to get cooking. I have embraced the mission; it's part of me and for the rest of the world. It's possible it will grow on you, too.

Ghana! Well, Tropical Ghana!

Born and raised in Ghana, history has it that I made my kitchen debut very early on in my life. As far as I can remember, I was always around food and the kitchen – for at least the first 20 years of my life. I grew up a farmer and a cook with my late uncle, Felix Brenya, an agriculturalist, and my aunt, Kate Okailey Brenya, a caterer. Many of my days were spent around animals, ingredients and food. If there were any out-of-the-ordinary skills that I had mastered by the age of 10, then it was chasing goats fiercely, aiming stones to pluck mangoes off the mango tree on first attempt, plus molding and baking bread in dozens.

I was a very curious kid who got to experience an enriched childhood and was afforded the opportunity to learn about the soil, animals, food crops, fruit trees, spices, food, cooking, everything food and, of course, food service; all in addition to going to school and picking up more skills as an everyday normal school kid. I worked alongside my late aunt as one of her catering assistants. It is from way back then that I picked my initial food skills and had the food experience added on that has been nurtured all these years to be part of my DNA.

When I think of it, it's easier now for me to sort of accept the name-calling and teasing by some of my friends during my childhood. These friends used interesting names such as "chicken handler," "goat chaser," "baker-o-baker," "cake boy," and many more. I did not take kindly to it back then. And I guaranteed those overzealous loudmouth friends no baked goodies during Christmas holidays whenever they went at me name-calling. Today, I can reach deep into my past experiences anytime to positively influence my daily activities. At that time though, I had a full schedule with everything food from the soil to the table, chasing animals and school. Though it might have seemed intense, I guess I was able to somehow manage it and have made it thus far. Thank God!

Years down the road, I am extremely grateful for my growing-up experience and how it has shaped me today as well as built my character and refined me in all of my endeavours. It is my exposure to farm life, fresh produce, ingredients, spices, flavours, animals, fresh-cooked food, family, friends, loved ones, inquisitive neighbours, going to school, books, life experiences and probably my closeness to the centre of the Earth in tropical Ghana that set the building blocks for the cooking project Tropical Ghana. Thank you to my late aunt and late uncle, parents, late grandparents, family, family friends, friends, teachers and loved ones for making my formative years on Earth truly worthwhile.

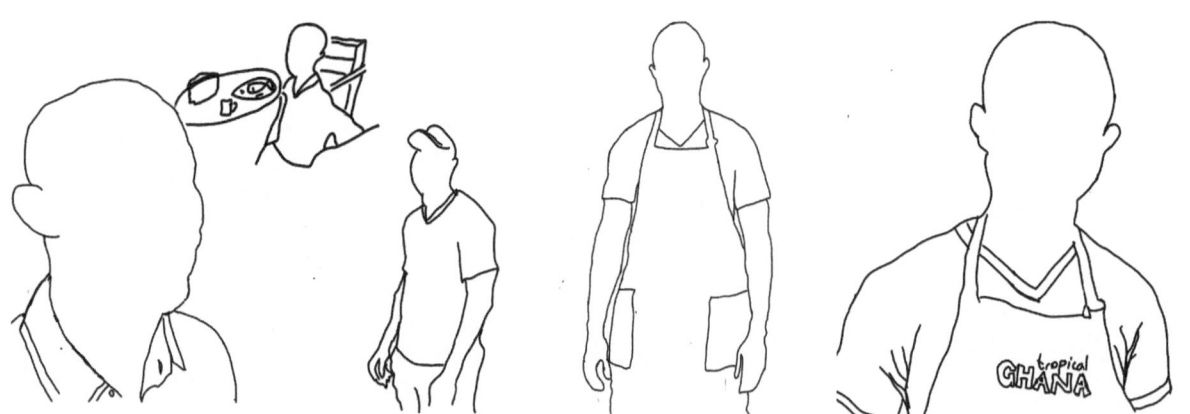

"

When families, friends and loved ones wake up every morning, I really want them to know that they have more options to eat nutritious and wholesome meals within their kitchen budgets with Tropical Ghana Kitchen Date.

"

Is Our Food Changing? Can We Still Eat Wholesome Now?

When I was growing up in Ghana, food was food – fresh, mouthwatering, delicious, natural, organic, tasty and full of life – as it should be. With the opportunity of living in other parts of the world and visiting other places, I have realized food is losing its special place. In order to enjoy ingredients and food that are naturally tasty, full of life or organic, chemical-free or what I always considered normal, you have to pay an arm and a leg in some parts of the world because of several reasons.

For me, it's really a sad reality that needs to change before it changes the whole world. If as human beings we erode our organic ingredients, then it will most likely affect our wholesome side, too, and chances are we shall not be able to continue to function as correctly and as fully as our bodies are designed. Without our organic, wholesome diets, we shall continue to be the biggest losers in the end. That should not be the case. Our diets are also becoming less and less wholesome or it keeps looking as if we are taking wholesomeness out of our diets.

How do we expect as humans to be completely whole and wholesome without any challenges to our body's infrastructure if we are not eating wholesome? This is a global challenge. My prayer is that, we can all eat nutritiously well, natural, organic, and keep it as wholesome as possible and maintain a balanced diet in our daily lives. And we should stand for and support farmers and food producers following sustainable, organic and chemical-free practices to get us our ingredients that keep our wholesome food journey on the right path.

When families, friends and loved ones wake up every morning, I really want them to know that they have more options to eat nutritious and wholesome meals within their kitchen budgets with *Tropical Ghana Kitchen Date*.

Generations Before Me

Growing up, weekends and holiday stays at my grandparents always had food playing a central role. I had the opportunity to spend loads and loads of time with my late grandmother and asked her several questions over the years about the food I grew up on in Ghana as well as how the food was two generations before me. I have also spoken to many other grandmothers, grandaunts and other women in my family and outside of my family, especially folks who have solid knowledge and understanding of food from where I come from. How can we get most of what we are losing back before it's too late? Can we and should we be guided by simple, fun and healthy steps that we can employ into our cooking?

The conversations, flavours, spices, aromas and ingredients got to me in a new way and ignited a unique way for me to approach the food I grew up on by maintaining all of its positives and wholesomeness. I cannot do much than to share all of the positive sides of Ghanaian cooking and more with you. Let's just say that's exactly what I am doing with Tropical Ghana. And that's why I am putting this special cookbook *Tropical Ghana Kitchen Date* out for you, too, to have some of the experiences from back in the day, around the time our grandmothers started cooking but in a new and exciting way that meets our appetite, our palate, our choices and our lifestyles of today.

Cooking Tropical Ghana style is the way I am bringing our world back to our wholesome side. It's the old-school way with a new positive energy and attitude. Our grandmothers nurtured their gardens and cooked food from scratch to finish in order to reap the full nourishment for their families. We cannot keep running around "in a hurry, somewhere" or "to do something" or "tapping screens nonstop." Slow down a bit to think of not only fresh and delicious, but also wholesome meals. My mission is to make cooking simple, fun and healthy for our current fast-paced generation, but at the same time to maintain high levels of wholesomeness as our mothers, grandmothers and great-grandmothers did generations before us. When I tell folks who attend cooking classes and workshops to forget their bankers and brokers, they laugh. But the best investment is cooking for yourself because you save so much cash and you know exactly what you are eating and what is going inside your body.

Tropical Ghana Kitchen Date is a food experience journey that will help bring the closest people around you even closer as you cook and share in a meal while at the same time inviting others who are not near to come close as we do in Ghana. Some will assume it's a community of food eaters. But I say, it's the way we are made as human beings to commune and have good, tasty food that leads to pure human interactions, conversations, and connections. In 2024, 18 years into Tropical Ghana's mission on this Earth, it easy to miss out on the magical human connections and interactions that make us function well because most of us are bombarded and or choked by so many activities as well as devices.

Years ago, I witnessed a friend's baby daughter, about three years of age, run and hug another toddler about her age. Out of the blue, the two ran and hugged so tightly right from when they saw each other from a distance. It was so natural and so organic that it blew me away. It was quite a sight! It felt as if the clock stopped. My friend marveled at the sight and so did every other person nearby around that time. We were caught up in a truly pure, human moment. Our human bond is getting lost. These two babies had never met prior to that encounter but it felt as if they had known each other for decades. The scenario spoke volumes to me. We can start cooking together once again as friends, family, loved ones, lovers and more to reignite our human bond once again even when we are long, long past the baby stages of our lives.

Inspired by the conversations, people, places, plants, fruits, herbs, animals, books, training, suggestions, tips, ingredients, spices, tastes, flavours, aromas, experiences, advice, food events, travels, and research that I am most grateful and thankful to have come across in my lifetime thus far, I present to you, *Tropical Ghana Kitchen Date*. It's my prayer that you and everyone around you will have a wonderful food experience with *Tropical Ghana Kitchen Date*!

As I continue the mission of Tropical Ghana, now is the time for all to come together and experience fresh meals from *Tropical Ghana Kitchen Date*. It's really the date you should really want! *Tropical Ghana Kitchen Date* is a clear assignment for those on a mission to have simple but good and delicious food in its freshness and wholesomeness with others. The assignment is food, and the mission is to see if you will settle for anything less after tasting Tropical Ghana recipes. I dare you! Let's eat a little better every day, from today, and invite others, too for a kitchen date with *Tropical Ghana Kitchen Date*!

#TropicalGhanaKitchenDate
#RediscoverYourTropicalSide
#RediscoverYourTropicalGhanaSide

Made with love, loads and loads of cooking, and smiles @TropicalGhana

GHANAIAN COOKING

Ghanaian cooking is a West African style cooking that mainly has a stew or soup paired and enjoyed with a carbohydrate staple such as Ghana Yam (West African Yam), plantain, sweet potato, Cassava, corn meal, and more. The stew or soup is made with vegetables such as tomatoes, onions, Scotch Bonnet, garlic, ginger, Okro (Okra), Garden Eggs, cocoyam leaves, and uniquely infused with a smoky flavour that is created by adding smoked fish or shrimp in granules or whole smoked fish plus fresh meats such as goat, chicken, beef, snails, fish, crabs and it is fully loaded with spices and delightful aromas.

Ghanaian cuisine is rich, textured, full of flavours, peppery, and with aromas that mark its unique identity on the world food map.

Ghana's culturally rich heritage is very evident in Ghanaian food, dishes, and recipes. In school, children do not only experience friends from various Ghanaian backgrounds, but also learn about other unfamiliar foods eaten in the other regions of the country they might not have visited but their classmates who come from those regions and areas tell them about the foods.

Ghana has five major ethnic groupings – the Akan, Ewe, Ga-Adangbe, Guan, and Mole Dagbani who all together add to the food landscape. Out of these five major ethnic groupings are smaller and other numerous cultural groupings and many, many languages with some that are uniquely standalones, others that are variants of the languages of major groups, while others are mixes and matches that have happened over time.

But one thing is for sure in Ghana: we are united by our stomachs! All of Ghana's ethnic and cultural groupings share Ghanaian food as a common unifier, bringing everyone together, both young and old, from far and near, and throughout the length and breadth of the country. Foods that originate in southern Ghana can be found in northern Ghana, and vice versa. In Ghana, our special investment is in our stomachs, and this brings us together in such a wonderful way.

Should anyone find him or herself in a major city such as the capital, Accra, or Kumasi, or Cape Coast, or Tamale, or Takoradi, or Sunyani, etc., tasting many of the foods and dishes of Ghana is possible. But for that lasting and unforgettable experience, making time to be in the locale known for the specific food or recipe or where its origins began will definitely be a blessing.

★ TROPICAL GHANA COOKING

Tropical Ghana cooking is a contemporary cooking style of combining traditional and non-traditional Ghanaian techniques by keeping the traditional roots, traits and taste of Ghanaian recipes while utilizing non-traditional cooking styles to make the recipes. The non-traditional approach is focused on simple, creative, and innovative cooking styles that harvest the natural qualities of each ingredient and retain the ingredients in their most fresh, potent, and wholesome state to be able to maximize the full potential of the nutrients in the recipe.

Imagine all of the positive sides of cooking from about three generations ago happening today, then taking that to the next level by utilizing the natural attributes of each of the ingredients in a recipe to harvest and maximize all the natural flavours produced by the ingredients. And then, elevate everything that's cooking to a whole new level of deliciousness. For instance, caramelizing an onion whether sliced, chopped or finely chopped in a recipe unlocks the natural onion sweetness that is harnessed into the cooked food to make it tastier.

In line with our contemporary style of cooking and celebrating each recipe's original roots, traits and taste, Tropical Ghana recipes have these characteristics:
- flavours created from unique herb mixtures
- ingredients added in ways to give food textural variety
- use minimum amounts of oil in recipes
- no preservatives, artificial flavouring, or additives
- no bouillon cubes

Ghana Welcomes You!
Some Ghanaian recipes may not be included here in this cookbook because the recipes cannot be celebrated in the way my ancestors would be proud of because of the respect for the unique, traditional way of making these dishes and the years involved in the gradual process of mastering the technique which is mostly handed down in families from generation to generation. Moreover, some of the ingredients are unique and not available in other regions of the world or the varieties that are available taste different compared to what you will find in Ghana. It's best described by a dedicated fan as "they don't taste the same outside Ghana." Please visit Ghana if you are missing any recipe not included here.

★ GHANAIAN FOOD & EXCITING PIECES THAT MARK ITS IDENTITY

Chop.

Small Chops in Ghana literally refers to finger foods or hors d'oeuvres. Like anywhere else in the world, finger foods or Small Chops excite most Ghanaians at gatherings, special occasions, parties, and events.

Come make we chop is an invite to join a friend to eat. This usually happens among close friends or family. When visiting a friend's home and the friend carries out a plate of food, the next thing you are likely to hear is "come make we chop" or "come make we chop errhh." It's a much more loving way of saying you are invited to join in the meal; and usually the feasting happens from the same plate which makes it even more special.

Chop – the word that wears many jackets in Ghana

Chop better is a phrase that gained traction in the late 1980s into the 90s when many citizens hoped for better lives from the economic pressures of the 1980s. As a hearty form of a tease and encouragement, "chop better" was openly said to friends to bring a smile to their faces in hopes of encouraging them that a better life is around the corner. It's also said out loud as a form of boast when any person has a special meal that is different from what they usually have on their daily plate.

Chop Bars in Ghana are places where people buy cooked food and sit to eat (chop). They are a traditional eatery of sorts without the glitz and glamour. Elements of Chop Bars come from the traditional way of eating in homes and in compound houses on short tables with stools and benches which started yesteryear in Ghanaian homes. They celebrate communal living, foster unity, and most agree the table height of the the stool helps anyone enjoy food much better.

Once a popular food fixture, Chop Bars are now slowly vanishing from the scene as many have evolved into contemporary eateries and restaurants. Only a few remaining ones in towns and villages are still maintaining their originalities. Nonetheless, they still present that down-to-earth communal African spirit witnessed around the table with smile upon smiles.

Chop time, no friend is a classic Ghanaian saying. Although most Ghanaians have an open heart and will share food, this is a saying to ward off potential intruders who want a piece that the person with the food is not willing to give. It's said into the open as a measure to notify all ears, though usually targeted at a specific person or persons so they do not even dream of "self-inviting" themselves. Also, this saying is often heard when sibling rivalry is at its peak.

Moreover, students in boarding schools and universities also rely on this very saying at crucial times. Around the end of the semester or term when final exams are ongoing and most students have their food supplies completely depleted, this saying reigns. A school mate who is completely out of food usually attempts to live off another friend's food supplies. But any person with plans to survive off his/her mate's food reserve will most likely come face to face with reality when they are stopped in their tracks with, "My friend, chop time, no friend!" It is rated as the best defense mechanism for students guarding their dwindling food supplies.

Asanka. Apotoyewa. Kaŋ.

Ghana's earthenware grinding bowl is the most recognizable cooking fixture across the length and breadth of the country. It's a unique grinding bowl made from clay with multiple lines etched in as a pattern inside that runs in different directions and acts as the "teeth" or blade or grinder that grinds, mashes, mixes vegetables, ingredients, herbs, spices and more.

The bowl has its own natural and organic way of tearing ingredients that are ground in it when its accompanying wooden masher is used to press the ingredients in the bowl. Moreover, it acts as a serving bowl for eating soups and other dishes. Found in almost every Ghanaian home, this unique bowl is also used in Chop Bars, eateries and restaurants to serve food. Locally, it known as Asanka or Apotoyewa/Ayewa (Twi language) and Kaŋ (Ga language).

Abele.

Abele (pronounced "ah-bay-lay") in the Ga language, and Eburo (pronounced "ebo-ro") in the Twi language, is the local name for maize or corn. Abele holds a major place in Ghanaian food and is used in numerous ways, playing a vital role in a typical week of most Ghanaians. So important is Abele that, one of Ghana's famed Highlife musicians, known as King of Highlife, the late ET Mensah, released a classical Highlife song titled "Abele."

The quality of a food or recipe made from Abele depends on the quality of the harvested Abele, the care used in cleaning and preparing it, the grinding or milling process and duration of fermentation if needed. The popular type of Abele in Ghana is similar to the varieties in other parts of West Africa that are much less water-laden white corn. Additionally, a handful of other colourful varieties are available.

The Ga-Adangbe people of Ghana on the coast know so much and have explored Abele to the extent that numerous recipes made from this prominent ingredient originally have Ga names. Food made from Abele such as Otimi or Komi (Kenkey), Banku, Abelemamu, Akpiti, Ashikoo, Eko Egbeimli, Oblaayo and more, hold names in the Ga language. Eaten fresh when harvested by boiling right away in water with the husk on or roasted with or without the husk, Abele has many other uses for food. Abele is soaked overnight, then milled in commercial grinders to use as wet corn meal, which is a key ingredient in many Ghanaian foods.

Shitɔ. Pepper.

Odjɛŋma

Kpakpo Shitɔ

Scotch Bonnet is known locally as **Odjɛŋma** (spelt also as Odzenma or Odjenma and pronounced "ojen-mma"). **Odjɛŋma** is a name from the Ga language which means "it smells good." Ŋma means good fragrance or something aromatic or an inviting scent. Basically, it's a pepper or chilli that adds a good aroma to cooking.

Market women in Ghana refer to it as scented pepper, and use slogans along those lines to attract more sales by doing the best to convince customers to add some fragrance to their cooking.

When Scotch Bonnet is unavailable, its cousin Habanero, which is widely available around the globe, can be used as a substitute. Scotch Bonnet has a sweet side, although it's a pepper with its heat high up on the pepper scale.

Kpakpo Shitɔ (pronounced "she-tor"), Pettie Belle Pepper or Pettie Belle Chilli, is popular in Ghana and found in other parts of West Africa. Kpakpo Shitɔ is a pepper that is smallish and almost round with probably a 3cm diameter. It has a sweet side but equally retains a decent pepper heat level that is well-loved for Ghanaian stews and soups.

Kpakpo Shitɔ plays a vital role when freshly ground together with onions and tomato in a clay grinding bowl and enjoyed with Kenkey and fish.

The name Kpakpo Shitɔ comes from its namesake Kpakpo, a male Ga name. Shitɔ means pepper in the Ga language. Basically, it is "Kpakpo's Pepper." It is believed once upon a time, Kpakpo Shitɔ was extremely loved by a man named Kpakpo, a true Ga man. We salute the original Kpakpo who has helped us all gain the same love for Kpakpo Shitɔ.

Akweley Waabii

Akweley Waabii (pronounced "ah-quay-lay wah-bee") which translates as Akweley's fingers is a Ga female name. The name is believed to have originated from a lady who famously kept her fingernails nice and colourful. Akweley Waabii is fresh Cayenne and also known also as Red Finger Hot Peppers in other regions of the world. Fresh Cayenne has its own unique character and plays its role in Ghanaian cooking.

Wele.

Wele (pronounced "way-lay") is preserved smoked cow hide. Wele is the one special ingredient that ends up in stews but has a nutritional value equal to zero. It is loved so much and believed to add a special flavour to food. Others are of the view that it is the feeling of biting into it, which is equal to none other, that they enjoy so much.

Fish & Salt.

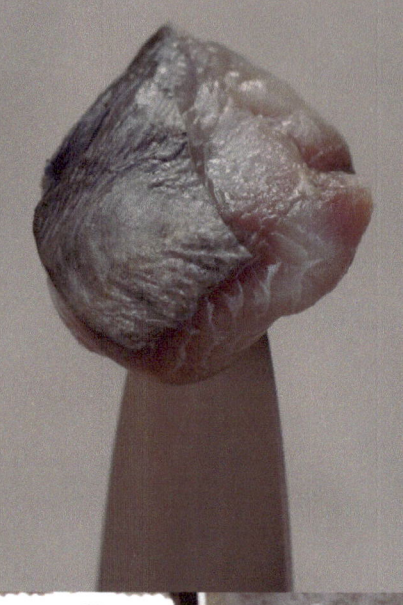

Loo Shala. Momoni. Stinking Fish.

Loo Shala (pronounced "low-sha-la") in the Ga language, or Momoni (pronounced "mor-mor-ni") in the Twi language, is Ghana's Stinking Fish. Yes, it has a real stink to it and will easily betray you if you try to hide it. Made with different kinds of fish such as Cassava Fish or Cassava Croaker, or Mackerel, the fish is scaled, gutted, rinsed, salted and allowed to ferment for days. Then it is salt-water washed, salted again, and partially dried for hours. At this point, it is ready for the market. All you need is a little piece added, especially fried into any stew that has palm oil as the base oil ingredient, and you will be amazed at the flavour. Lightly rinse it before use to clean and reduce the salt content.

Koobi.

Koobi, sun-dried salted Tilapia, is another important ingredient in Ghanaian food. Fresh Tilapia is scaled, gutted with gills left, rinsed, and heavily salted, then sun-dried for days to thoroughly dry. Good Koobi is a very well-dried Koobi. The way Koobi is preserved with salt makes the dried fish retain most of the salt even after a light rinse with water. When used in a stew, no salt should be added because Koobi contains enough salt.

Keta School Boys.

Keta School Boys are sun-dried salted anchovies. With such a unique name, this ingredient is a real delicacy which clearly gained popularity first from its namesake place – Keta (pronounced "kay-tah"), in the Volta Region of Ghana. Fresh anchovies are rinsed with water, salted and sun-dried for days to thoroughly dry. Before use, place amount to be used in a bowl of water to rinse. Pick it out of the water so any particles or foreign debris settles at the bottom of the bowl. Shake off excess water with a sieve. Dry-pan toasting for a few minutes is a good way to warm it up.

Groundnuts & Groundnut Paste.

Groundnuts from Ghana are some of the tastiest of what is known as peanuts in other parts of the world. Groundnuts are nuts that come from the ground hence their very simple name in Ghana. In its shell, it can be boiled in water with salt and enjoyed as a snack. Nevertheless, it is more popular when out of the shell and dry-pan toasted or roasted using mastered traditional techniques of adding some sea sand which naturally adds salt while at the same time extracting excess oil. The end result is well-roasted unblanched groundnuts that can make you smile. Groundnut Paste is made when roasted groundnut are ground into a smooth paste with no additives. It does a perfect job primarily as a spread on bread. Additionally, groundnuts are a main component in Ghana's well-known Groundnut Soup that delights more than a thousand.

Oven-Dried Smoked Fish & Shrimp.

The unique, smoky flavour in Ghanaian cooking comes from no other place than dried fish and shrimp added whole, in pieces or mostly in powdered form. The widely-known smoke flavour is added during the oven-drying process from firewood that is used.

Herrings are the most preferred fish in Ghana's dried fish powder. Dried shrimp powder features equally in this department. Some people like to combine both fish and shrimp powder in stews and more. Whether with fish, or shrimp, or both, using these ingredients will help you attain one of the flavours of Ghanaian cooking

Fish Powder

Shrimp Powder

Gari.

Ghana's Gari is crispy dry-pan toasted dried granules of Cassava (Yuca) that is created when Cassava is grated or ground in a mill and taken through a few drying steps. Prior to dry-pan toasting, the grated Cassava is placed into bags and pressured under weights in order to remove excess liquid starch and speed dehydration.

This desiccation process also initiates a very light form of fermentation. From this step, the grated dried Cassava is introduced into a pan and gently dry-toasted. Over time, it shrinks and takes its own shape that ends up as dry, crispy granules.

Gari can be eaten raw in very small amounts or added to various Ghanaian and West African dishes. It's a nice addition when eating with Red Red as it adds a special touch. A good-tasting Gari comes from the quality of the Cassava in terms of its freshness and tastiness, the size of the grated Cassava, the amount of liquid starch removed, and the overall perfection of the pan-toasting process.

Gari-making is a skill mastered by families, and these family techniques are passed on from generation to generation. Once you find a good Gari supplier that meets your perfect taste, you stick to that supplier or that family for your Gari needs. Gari should not be confused with thin-sliced pickled ginger served with sushi that sounds the same and with a similar spelling.

Zomi & Zomi-Under.

Zomi is spiced palm oil. Palm oil is widely available in Ghana, but the spiced version takes palm oil to a whole new special level. Spiced with ginger, garlic, onions, various peppers, herbs and more, the palm oil undergoes an infusion process which includes frying and other secret techniques to churn Zomi.

When the process is complete, all the spices used in the creation leaves a highly-coveted tasty debris that settles at the bottom known as Zomi Shishi (Ga) or Zomi Asie (Twi). The basic closest translation to English is Zomi-Under. This sediment is priceless and used in small amounts together with Zomi to enjoy Red Red and for stews that have palm oil as an ingredient.

Dzomi/Zomi

Zomi-Under

Zomi-Under on beans

Like Gari, one must have a trusted Zomi producer who knows the art form well from his or her family's closely-guarded top secret recipe. It is no secret that the best Dzomi or Zomi comes from trusted families and producers in the Volta Region of Ghana. Beware of regular palm oil disguised as Zomi.

Item 13.

During a period of time in Ghana's history, and especially when official functions such as conferences, workshops, and events were held, the agenda or order of the programme always featured refreshments listed as "point number 13 or item 13." This made it become "the thing" that everyone looks out for and looks forward to at all events.

Over time, "Item 13" became renowned as a reference for food, eating, or getting refreshments, or the like, at gatherings in Ghana.

Common Dry Spices.

Black Peppercorns | West African Black Pepper | Wie Din (Ga) | Esoro Wisa (Twi)

Grains of Paradise | Alligator Pepper Guinea Pepper | Wie Tsuru/Tsulu (Ga) Efom Wisa (Twi)

Grains of Selim | Ethiopian Pepper So (Ga) | Hwentia (Twi)

Cloves | Dadoa Amba | Pɛprɛ (Twi) Mbrɛgo Amba (Fante)

Anise Seeds | Osu Kon (Ga) Nkitikiti (Twi)

Calabash Nutmeg African Orchid Nutmeg Mlia (Ga) | Wede Aba (Twi)

Others & Others.

Star Anise

Prekese | Aridan Fruit

Dried Hibiscus Flowers
Sobolo | Bissap | Sorrel

Boabab Powder

One Very Special Condiment.

Shitɔ Din. Black Shitɔ.

Shitɔ Din (Black Shitɔ) is a very special thickly prepared pepper mix that everybody loves. Those who know how to make it know how to make it. They do not talk much because many out there claim to be experts but upon tasting their version, you might be disappointed.

The combination of peppers, onions, garlic, ginger, other herbs and spices plus shrimp and fish powder fried down into this delicious condiment needs training under the tutelage of an experienced maker. It is one of those secrets that is carried within families and passed onto all those who are willing to learn the craft and maintain the quality.

One Very Special Kitchen Set.

Mortar & Pestle

Mortar & Pestle is another essential pair in Ghanaian cooking. The most popular one is the large one with a flat bottom used for pounding and making fufu. Another version with a concave bottom is second in line and a workhorse for spices, nuts, and mainly used for anything dry that needs to be turned into powder.

Made with wood, both versions have evolved and currently table top varieties are available.

★ ══════ INGREDIENTS AROUND THE WORLD & SIMPLE MEASURING

Beginning with the little kid, boy or girl making his or her kitchen debut, to the adult doing a comeback or continuing in his or her craft, or grandma or grandpa simply imparting some useful cooking wisdom on the next generation, these recipes are simple and straight-forward to follow.

Clean Hands! Clean Kitchen! Clean Ingredients!
Before working around food or cooking a recipe, kindly wash your hands thoroughly with soap. Always keep your kitchen or cooking area tidy, cleaning the floor regularly, always wiping surfaces and cleaning tools and equipment. Once you have your fresh ingredients, make sure to wash everything thoroughly with water, and in cases of fruits and vegetable with skin and leaves that will be consumed, please pay particular attention to wash and rinse them well.

Ingredients are listed with a close substitute next to it to help anyone get going right away. See an example below:
> – Scotch Bonnet (Habanero) pepper

This means the main ingredient is Scotch Bonnet, but it can be substituted by Habanero which is its cousin from the same family. And Habanero might be what's available in the region of the world you find yourself because the original ingredient is not readily available or cannot be sourced. Most of the recipes in this cookbook have ingredients listed in this similar way.

Onions are widely used in Ghanaian cooking, so in this cookbook:
> – A small onion is approximately 4oz–5oz (113g–142g)
> – A medium onion is approximately 6oz–8oz (170g–227g)
> – A large onion is approximately 10oz–12oz (283g–340g)

Measurements go from teaspoons, to tablespoons, to ounces, to cups, to grams, to millilitres, to other accepted forms of measuring units that are universal.
See examples:
> – 8 tbsp (4fl oz/125ml) palm oil
> – 2 cups (10½oz/300g) flour

Tablespoon and teaspoons equivalent

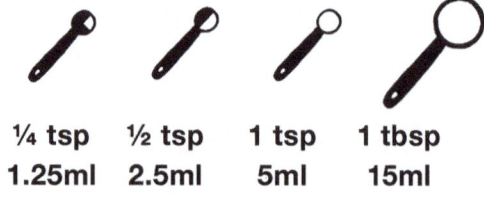

¼ tsp	½ tsp	1 tsp	1 tbsp
1.25ml	2.5ml	5ml	15ml

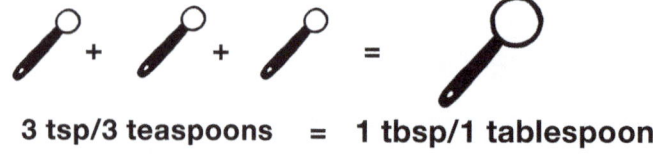

3 tsp/3 teaspoons = 1 tbsp/1 tablespoon

Liquid Measure Equivalents

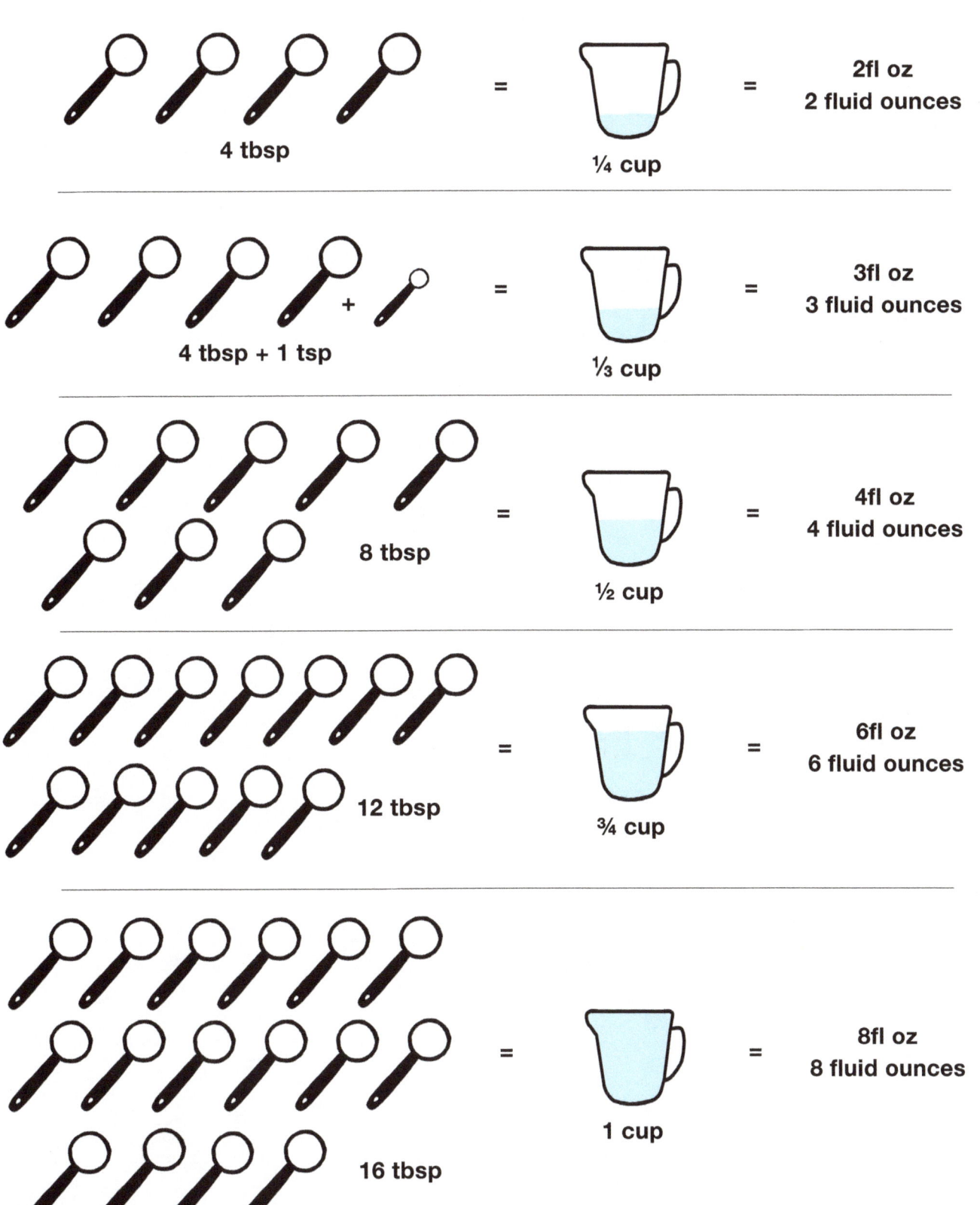

4 tbsp = ¼ cup = 2fl oz / 2 fluid ounces

4 tbsp + 1 tsp = ⅓ cup = 3fl oz / 3 fluid ounces

8 tbsp = ½ cup = 4fl oz / 4 fluid ounces

12 tbsp = ¾ cup = 6fl oz / 6 fluid ounces

16 tbsp = 1 cup = 8fl oz / 8 fluid ounces

MOVERS & SHAKERS

Movers & Shakers are loaded with the ingredients needed to zoom straight to the various departments in your body that need them the most. Shake things up a bit and move things in the right direction towards that healthier lifestyle.

Tropical Coleslaw

Serves: 8 | **Prep Time:** 15 minutes | **Salad Time:** 10 minutes

By popular request, a coleslaw with a bit more oomph. So, we did it! Tropical Coleslaw adds a bit more colour and flavour to the classic coleslaw to brighten all of the days of all coleslaw lovers and attempt to keep them focused on any task ahead.

For Salad

- 1 head cabbage, washed, pat dry, finely chopped
- 3 large carrots, washed, pat dry, curled with a peeler into 2½ inch ribbons

For Topping

- 1 large mango, peeled and cut into half inch cubes
- 8 mint leaves, chiffonade

For Dressing

- 2 tbsp mayonnaise
- 4 tsp red wine vinegar
- 1 tbsp olive oil
- ¼ tsp black pepper
- ¼ tsp salt
- ½ tangerine, juiced
- ½ lime, zest

Preparation

1. Mix shredded cabbage and carrots in a large salad bowl.

2. In a small bowl, combine mayonnaise, red wine vinegar, olive oil, tangerine juice, salt and pepper. Whisk to mix completely and spread over cabbage and carrots.

3. Toss with a serving spoon. Blitz with lime zest.

4. Top with mango cubes and mint leaves.

> **Tip: Go the extra step**
> Take the Tropical Coleslaw to the new tropical level and toss in some freshly chopped cauliflower florets after adding mango.

37

Tropical Greeno Coleslaw

Serves: 8 | **Prep Time:** 15 minutes | **Salad Time:** 15 minutes

For Greeno Dressing

- 10 cauliflower florets, rinsed
- ¼ avocado, freshly cut
- 1 tbsp red wine vinegar
- 1 tbsp olive oil
- ¼ tsp cayenne pepper
- ¼ tsp salt
- ½ tangerine, juiced
- ½ lime, juice

For Quick Blanch Cauliflower Florets

- 1 tbsp water
- 1 cup iced water

For Salad

- Follow the steps for making a Tropical Coleslaw

Tropical Coleslaw goes up a division to heavy-weight – just kidding. It's simply gone full-on vegetarian with the introduction of the Greeno dressing. Greeno is for all who love something else that's not mayo in their coleslaw. Greeno is a real green substitute for mayo from vegetables and fruits. Add Greeno to the Tropical Coleslaw and get your Tropical Greeno Coleslaw. It might be a good idea to keep it a secret.

Greeno Dressing Preparation

1. Add a tablespoon of water to cauliflower florets in pan over high heat for 3 minutes. Immediately remove cauliflower florets into a cup of iced water for 2 minutes to cool off.

2. Add quarter avocado, red wine vinegar, olive oil, cayenne pepper, salt and tangerine juice in blender. Top with cauliflower florets. Blitz into a paste.

3. Pour Greeno dressing into a bowl. Squeeze juice of half lime and stir to mix completely.

4. Top with fresh zest of lime and add as dressing for Tropical Coleslaw or other salads of choice.

Alternately, zest lime on Tropical Coleslaw after mixing with dressing and plating.

5. Salad away into a tropical green state of mind!

Tip: Go the extra step

Take the Tropical Coleslaw to the new tropical level and toss in some freshly chopped cauliflower florets after adding mango.

Greeno Dressing

Looks like guacamole but don't let the green colour trick you.

It's simply a Greeno, a true vegetable and fruit mix substitute for those who want something that is not mayo.

Cucumber On Date Salad

Serves: 6 | **Prep Time:** 15 minutes | **Salad Time:** 5 minutes

If cucumber had a chance to go on a date, who would it be with? What if cucumber had a Tropical Ghana Kitchen Date? Here's to discovering cucumber's side that's less often seen and everything else that adds to make cucumber's first real date very special. This is a salad with a refreshing natural sweetness for all lovers of cucumber who want to go on a date.

For Main Salad Mix

• 4 small cucumbers, washed, freshly chopped

• 1 bunch fresh Dino kale, trimmed, washed, pat dry, finely chopped or chiffonade

• 6 spring onions (scallions), cleaned, white part freshly chopped

Tip: Add almonds
Top with toasted sliced almonds if you love almonds.

Preparation

1. Mix chopped cucumber, Dino kale, and spring onion whites in a large salad bowl.

2. In a blender, combine dates, tangerine juice and pulp, red wine vinegar, olive oil, teaspoon and half ginger, slice of red sweet pepper and salt. Blitz to mix completely into salad dressing and spread over cucumber, kale, and spring onion mix.

3. Toss with a serving spoon and plate salad.

4. Top with slices dates, sliced Akweley Waabii (fresh cayenne) and pan-toasted Agusi or toasted pumpkin seeds.

For Date Dressing

For Date Dressing
- 4 dates
- 1 tangerine, seeded, pulp and juice
- 4 tsp red wine vinegar
- 1 tbsp olive oil
- 1½ tsp ginger, freshly minced
- a slice of red sweet pepper/ red bell pepper
- ¼ tsp salt

For Topping
- 1 Akweley Waabii (red finger hot pepper/fresh cayenne), seeded, washed, sliced
- 4 dates, sliced
- 2 tsp Agushi/Egusi (melon seeds or pumpkin seeds); dry-pan toasted

Highlife Salad

Serves: 6 | **Prep Time:** 10 minutes | **Salad Time:** 10 minutes

"Highlife Salad helps ignite that music in you, so you can shout and dance from your innermost parts for the gift of life."

Highlife music is Ghana's foremost recognizable and popular music genre before and after independence. It's the one genre of music that is not only truly Ghanaian, but also truly West African and hits all the right spots if you can spot it, simmer it, and move to it.

Sometimes, there's that music that's deep inside the soul with a rhythm and a beat that expresses the sense of gratitude for the gift of life to see another day. It is such an indescribable, genuine sense that make you reach a high or height of joy to be alive and be really grateful for God's blessing. It's like your inside is dancing to some music and the music sounds very similar to a good Ghanaian Highlife tune.

The way the different musical instruments are combined is similar to the way ingredients can be combined to give you that rhythm, beat, melody and more.

Presenting to the world an original that highlights the signature style of Tropical Ghana recipes, Highlife Salad helps ignite that music in you, so you can shout and dance from your innermost parts for the gift of life. It's a salad inspired by the Ghanaian music genre and packed with the enjoyment of a good, old tune.

Highlife Salad is the joy of the gift of life with grace from above and freshly loaded with what the earth has to offer for you to stay on the good highs of life with good nutrients as well as some good music. Do invite others to be part of this! experience.

   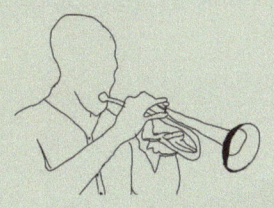 

Dandelion Greens

Carrot Ribbons

Spring Onion Whites

Coconut Chips

Chopped Mango

For Salad

• 1 bunch fresh dandelion greens, washed, trimmed, cut to bite-sized pieces
• 2 carrots, cleaned and curled with a peeler into 2½inch length ribbons
• 3 spring onions (scallions), cleaned, white part freshly chopped
• 4oz lightly sweetened toasted coconut chips
• 1 ripe mango, peeled and chopped

For Topping

• 8 grape tomatoes, halved
• 1 avocado, peeled, sliced

For Mango Vinaigrette

• 2 tbsp wine vinegar
• 2 tbsp olive oil
• 3 tbsp chopped mango
• 1 small Akweley Waabii (red finger hot pepper/fresh cayenne)
• pinch of salt

Preparation

1. In a large bowl, combine dandelion greens, carrot ribbons, spring onion whites, coconut chips and mango. Gently toss with serving spoon.

2. Combine all of the ingredients for the vinaigrette in a blender. Blend for about 30 seconds.

3. Plate salad and top with grape tomato halves and avocado slices.

4. Drizzle plated salads with the vinaigrette and grab a plate to enjoy.

> **Tip: Keep it fresh!**
> Don't drizzle with vinaigrette till you are ready to serve and eat.

Sunset Salad

Serves: 6 | Prep Time: 10 minutes | Salad Time: 10 minutes

Sunsets are lovely, but catching a tropical sunset can give that lovely, warm, cozy end of day feeling. Sunset Salad is a warm salad that brings a touch of that that delightful, end-of-day warmth. A straightforward, simple salad to kick back and admire nature slow down.

For Golden Onion
- 1 large yellow onion (10oz/284g), sliced, onion ring style
- 2 tbsp olive oil
- ¾ tsp salt

For Main Salad Mix
- 1 bunch fresh Dino kale, washed, trimmed, cut to bite-sized pieces
- 3 carrots, washed, peeled, halved lengthwise, cut on a diagonal

For Topping
- 1 red bell pepper (red sweet pepper), de-seeded, freshly sliced rings

Preparation

1. In a saucepan combine oil, yellow onion slices, and salt over high heat for about 5–7 minutes, stirring continuously.

2. Add carrots to sizzling yellow onion when onion bits soften and begin to turn golden brown on the edges. Stir for another a minute or two. Turn off heat.

3. Add Dino kale mix completely.

4. Plate this warm salad and top with red bell pepper rings.

> **Tip: More colours**
> Add yellow, orange, and green bell peppers for more colour.

Green Bean Salad

Serves: 4 | Prep Time: 12 minutes | Salad Time: 10 minutes

Are the kids eating their greens? Or are they playing to avoid it? Green Bean Salad is a Tropical Ghana signature salad that is truly refreshing. It's a quick, light and colourful salad option that can easily attract kids to the table. If you are thinking of going green with the kids, go together in style and with a little more colour with Green Bean Salad.

For Salad

- 1lb (16oz/454g) green beans, trimmed and rinsed
- 2 carrots, washed, peeled, julienned
- 1 hard ripe mango, peeled and julienned
- 8 grape tomatoes, halved
- 6 tbsp water

For Dressing

- 1 tangerine

> **Tip: Enjoy green beans with steam**
> Skip the ice bath and pour steamed green beans into a large salad bowl to finish salad.

Preparation

1. Bring water to boil in a saucepan over medium heat. Add green beans and cover with lid to steam for 3–5 minutes only. The green beans absorb all the water within the 3–5 minute timeframe.

2. Meanwhile, prepare an ice bath by placing ice cubes in a bowl with water.

3. Pour green beans into a colander. Immerse the colander with steamed green beans into a bowl with ice cubes. The ice bath cools the beans fast and helps retain the pristine green color by eliminating the heat.

4. After 5 minutes, remove green beans from ice bath, and shake colander to drain excess water. Place in a salad bowl, add mango and carrots, and gently toss.

5. Spritz with fresh tangerine juice, garnish with halved grape tomatoes, and serve.

6. Enjoy this salad and be inspired by the colors of nature.

APPETIZERS, STARTERS, WARMERS, ICE BREAKERS & GATHER-AROUND-KIDS

Break the ice with some bites that come with a munch or a crunch to help start conversations. And these conversations often happen with strangers who are also on a snack mission. Get the kids excited for some delicious snacks.

Introducing the new appetizing class of 2024

New York Ginger Mint Coookies With Honey Yogurt.
A cookie recipe with Ghanaian roots but a New York City attitude.

Rhythm & Beet Smoothie.
The pick-me-up for those off-beat days.

Aluguntugui Delight.
A tropical drink with a refreshing citrus splash.

Baked Koose.
A popular street joy in a slightly newer jacket.

Cocoa Plantain.
When Cocoa meets Plantain, the love story.

Sobolo Mango Smoothie.
A smoothie with Sobolo DNA but full of mango's playfulness.

New York Ginger Mint Cookies With Honey Yogurt

Serves: 12 | **Prep Time:** 15 minutes | **Baking Time:** 25 minutes

For Cookies
- 2 cups (10½oz/300g) flour
- 3 tbsp sugar
- 2 tbsp vegetable oil
- 4 tbsp margarine
- ½ tsp salt
- ½ tsp baking powder
- 1 egg
- 2 tsp vanilla extract
- 4 tbsp ginger, freshly minced
- 12 mint leaves, finely chopped
- ½ orange, zest and juiced

For Yogurt Mix
- 8oz plain yogurt of choice
- 1 mango, peeled, finely chopped
- 2 tbsp dried cranberries
- 8 mint leaves, chiffonade
- 3oz bag sweet plantain chips

For Topping
- 3 tbsp honey
- 1 plumcot or Anjou pear or apple

Tip: Use your fresh fruit of choice.

Preparation

1. Preheat oven to 375°F (190°C/Gas 5).

2. Combine sugar, oil, margarine, salt, egg, vanilla, ginger, mint, orange zest and juice with an electric mixer at medium speed for about 2 minutes or beat with whisk for about 5 minutes in a large bowl.

3. Add flour and baking powder and mix thoroughly into cookie dough.

4. Lightly grease baking sheets. Scoop teaspoon full of dough and press into baking sheet with teaspoon to about 1/8inch (3mm) thickness, repeat till baking sheet is filled. Or use a rolling pin to roll dough to about 1/8inch (3mm) or desired thickness and cut out shapes with cookie cutters or pastry cutters of choice.

5. Place in oven and let bake for about 20–25 minutes, or until golden brown and done. Remove and let cool for about 7–10 minutes.

6. As cookies' cool, prepare yogurt mix by combining yogurt, mango, dried cranberries, and mint in a bowl. Mix thoroughly. Crush plantain chips in bag with a heavy tea mug and add to yogurt mix as desired.

7. Scoop a teaspoon full of yogurt mix onto each baked cookie, top with slices of plumcot or Anjou pear or apple or fresh fruit of choice in your region, then drizzle with honey and serve.

Tropical Ghana Meat Pies

Serves: 25 | **Prep Time:** 45 minutes | **Baking Time:** 25 minutes

Tropical Ghana Meat Pies are finger foods that keep the conversations up and ideas alive. Though a snack, it always draws crowds even when snack break is over. Popularly called Meat Pies in Ghana but made with different fillings of chicken, beef, fish, other meats, vegetables and more, these pies easily fit in the palm and slide quickly into the mouth. Making these delicious pies can be a breeze when you have all hands on deck to help, so rope in any family or friends around.

For Pastry Mix
- 9 cups (42oz/1.2kg) all-purpose flour
- 1¼lbs (20oz/567g) margarine
- 6oz (170g) vegetable shortening
- 10 tsp olive oil
- 1 tsp salt
- 1½ tsp baking powder
- ¾ cup (6fl oz/177ml) iced water

For Rolling Pastry
- 4 tbsp flour

For Brushing Pastry
- 4 tbsp/¼ cup (2fl oz/60ml) milk

For Pie Filling
- 1lb (16oz/454g) minced beef sirloin
- 1 sweet potato (10oz/283g), peeled, finely chopped
- 1 medium carrot, cleaned, finely chopped
- 1 medium red onion (6oz/170g), finely chopped
- 30 fresh basil leaves, freshly chopped
- 4 tsp ginger, freshly minced
- 4 cloves garlic, finely chopped
- 1 tsp black pepper
- 1 tbsp olive oil
- 1 tsp salt

Preparation

1. Make pastry by combining flour, salt and baking powder in a food processor. Pulse on and off for a few seconds to mix completely. Add margarine, vegetable shortening and olive oil. Pulse on and off for about 5 minutes to mix to a texture that leaves tiny margarine bits about the size of a grain of corn.

Alternatively, a pastry blender or your fingers can be used in the absence of a food processor to blend in and mix margarine, vegetable shortening, olive oil and dry ingredients. This method might require an additional 5–8 minutes for thorough mix.

2. Slowly add iced water in small amounts as you keep pulsing on and off in food processor or mixing with your fingers until dough comes together and begins to stick. Form 4 dough balls. Place dough balls in bowl with a cover. Cover and refrigerate in freezer for at least 10–15 minutes or chill in fridge overnight.

3. In a saucepan, add beef, olive oil, half of finely chopped onions, garlic, and half a teaspoon of black pepper as well as a teaspoon of minced ginger.

4. Partially cook over high heat, stirring continuously for about 5–7 minutes. Using a folk, flake beef as necessary to prevent lumps from forming as it precooks. Turn heat off as soon as beef color starts changing from pink to brown. Let cool for 5 minutes, leaving saucepan uncovered.

5. As beef cools, prep 2 baking sheets by brushing lightly with a teaspoon of oil and lightly dust with flour.

6. Add the rest of the onions, ginger, black pepper plus sweet potato, carrot, basil and salt to cooled beef mix. Mix completely into a colorful pie filling.

7. Using a rolling pin, roll out pastry close to 1/8inch (3mm) thickness on lightly floured surface. Use a small dough press or a mini pie mold or a round cookie cutter, about 3–4 inches in diameter, for cutting rolled pastry. Dip cutter or mold in pastry flour, press on pastry, and stamp out round shapes. Fill each shape with about 1 teaspoon full of pie filling.

8. Brush the edges with water and fold over, along the diameter, to create a half moon shape. Press down on the edges with your finger; the water will make the edges stick together easily. Repeat until all pastry is used.

9. Preheat oven to 450°F (230°C/Gas 8).

10. Place pies on baking sheets. Using a fork or a table knife, punch holes on the mini pie tops to serve as air pockets during baking. Brush pie tops with milk before placing in the oven. The milk gives it a baked, golden brown finish.

11. Place in oven for 5 minutes and then reduce heat to 375°F (190°C/Gas 5). Let bake for about 20–25 minutes. Rotate tray at least once during baking time for even baking on all sides. Let bake until tops are golden brown. Remove and place pies on cooling racks.

12. Serve this finger food hot and let the meat pies inspire your day.

> **Tip: Try with minced turkey or fish!**
> Use minced turkey instead of beef. Alternatively, mix and match half beef, half lamb or half chicken, half turkey or minced pork. Or try it with your favorite fresh fish like fillet Grouper, Tilapia, or a mix. When using fresh fish, do not precook; fillet and finely chop fish and you are ready to start the pie journey.

Bofrot/Boflot

Serves: 10 | **Prep Time:** 2–3 hours | **Frying Time:** 25 minutes

For Flour Mix
- 4 cups (21oz/600g) all-purpose flour, plus extra for dusting
- 5 tbsp (2.1oz/60g) brown sugar
- ½ tsp salt
- 2 tsp nutmeg
- 2 tsp (7g) yeast
- 4 tbsp margarine

For Liquids
- 1 tsp vanilla essence/extract
- ¼ cup (2fl oz/60ml) milk
- ¾ cup (6fl oz/177ml) warm water

For Frying
- 5 cups (40oz/1.2L) vegetable oil

Preparation

1. In a large bowl, combine flour, sugar, salt, nutmeg, yeast, and mix thoroughly.

2. Make a well in the center and add margarine into it. Add milk, warm water, and vanilla essence. Starting from the inside of well and moving outward, bring the dry ingredients into the warm water and mix all together until it forms into a dough. Lightly dust a table with flour and knead dough for about 5 minutes, to smooth the dough and remove any air pockets.

Alternatively, an electric mixer with a dough hook can be used to mix the dough.

3. Divide dough into about 20 equal sizes and shape into balls about the size of a ping pong ball. Place on a tray dusted with extra flour. Leave in a warm place for about 2–3 hours to proof or when each ball shape doubles in size.

4. Heat oil in a large deep-frying pan over medium heat. To check and confirm oil is hot for frying to begin, gently drop a small piece of lemon or orange rind in the oil. The lemon or orange rind will immediately rise from the bottom of the pan to the top and start browning. Or use a piece of bread, which will turn golden in seconds. Pick out the rind or bread and discard.

5. Gently drop each dough ball into oil. Fry for about 7–12 minutes or until all sides are deep golden brown. Turn Bofrot a few times during the frying time with a large slotted spoon to have all sides golden brown.

6. Remove Bofrot with the large slotted spoon into a mesh sieve or mesh strainer for about 5 minutes to drain excess oil. Transfer to plate or tray lined with kitchen paper or paper towel to continue draining any extra oil.

7. Repeat process till all of the dough balls are fried.

8. The Bofrot is ready and best when enjoyed hot as is or with a drink.

> **Tip: Even frying and better results**
> Use a heavy-duty or thick base deep-frying pan or saucepan for even distribution of the heat for better results Bofrot.

Toogbei

Serves: 10 | Prep Time: 30 minutes | Frying Time: 25 minutes

For Flour Mix
• 4 cups (21oz/600g) all-purpose flour
• 5 tbsp (2.1oz/60g) brown sugar
• ½ tsp salt
• 1 tsp nutmeg, grated
• 4 tsp (14g) dry yeast
• 2½ tsp margarine
• 1 tsp olive oil (vegetable oil)

For Liquid Mix
• 2¾ cups (22fl oz/680ml) warm water

For Frying
• 5 cups (40oz/1.2L) vegetable oil

Preparation

1. In a large bowl, combine flour, sugar, salt, nutmeg, yeast, and mix thoroughly.

2. Make a well in the center and add margarine and olive oil into the well. Add warm water. Starting from inside of well and moving outward, bring the dry ingredients into the warm water and mix all together until it forms into a sticky dough. The hand is best used for mixing this very sticky dough.

Alternatively, an electric mixer on low with a dough hook can be used to mix the dough or use a wooden spoon.

3. Cover with a damp cloth. Leave in a warm place for about 30 minutes to prove dough or until dough doubles in size.

4. Heat oil in a large deep-frying pan over medium heat. To check and confirm oil is hot for frying to begin, gently drop a small piece of lemon or orange rind in the oil. The lemon or orange rind will immediately rise from the bottom of the pan to the top and start browning. Or use a piece of bread, which will turn golden in seconds. Pick out the rind or bread and discard.

5. The hand is traditionally used to scoop a sizeable amount while the palm aids in shaping it round to about a ping pong ball size before gently dropping into the oil.

Alternatively, use an ice cream scoop or tabespoon. Dip in water, scoop, and shape dough, then gently drop into oil. Add one scoop at a time, do not overcrowd frying pan.

6. Fry for about 7–12 minutes or until all sides are deep golden brown. Turn Toogbei a few times during the frying time with a large slotted spoon, making sure all sides are golden brown.

7. Remove Toogbei with the large slotted spoon into a mesh sieve or mesh strainer for about 5 minutes to drain excess oil. Transfer to plate or tray lined with kitchen paper or paper towel to continue draining any extra oil.

8. Repeat process till the dough runs out. Enjoy Toogbei hot with friends and family.

Baked Koose/Ghana Baked Beans

Serves: 12 | **Prep Time:** 4 hours or overnight | **Baking Time:** 35 minutes

Koose (pronounced "koh-say") is a deep-fried street food snack made out of whipped black eye beans batter. A breakfast item that excites most Ghanaians in the morning as well as a tasty snack to munch on at any time of the day, Koose is also known as Akara in Nigeria and has been around for centuries. It is believed to have made its way to Brazil as Acaraje – a popular Brazilian street food – during the slave trade.

In Ghana, this delicious, vegetarian West African treat pairs very well with Hausa Koko – a millet porridge infused with spices or Mah Koko – a corn porridge. Koose is full of so much goodness that it's time to send it off to the next level. A newer, healthier form is born and joins the family at Tropical Ghana. It is the Ghana Baked Beans. Enter Baked Koose! It's the next generation in the Koose family that retains the wholesomeness of the beans to get you recharging right away.

For Soaking Beans

- 1 cup (8oz/227g) black eye beans
- 2½ cups (20fl oz/600ml) water

For Koose Mix

- 1 red finger hot pepper (fresh cayenne)
- ½ red bell pepper (red sweet pepper), de-seeded
- 1 small (4oz/113g) yellow onion
- 1 tsp salt
- 1 tsp Zomi (spiced palm oil)
- 3 pieces Calabash Nutmeg (½ nutmeg)
- 2oz (57g) ginger root, peeled
- 1 cup (8fl oz/237ml) water

> **Tip 1: Check beans for "extras" and anything foreign**
> It's important to carefully examine beans when in use in any recipe to pick out anything other than the beans, such as bits of chaff, small stones or particles. Rinse and you are on your way to making a great bean recipe.

> **Tip 2: Is it baked?**
> A toothpick can be inserted into Koose to check if it is baked. The toothpick comes out clean without any wet bean mix if completely baked.

Preparation

1. Pour beans on a tray and spend about 5 minutes or less to carefully pick out anything other than the beans, such as bits of chaff, small stones or particles.

2. Rinse beans with water and use colander to drain excess water. Place rinsed beans in a large bowl with cover or cooking pot and add 2½ cups of water. Cover and leave overnight or for at least 4 hours for beans to absorb water.

3. Preheat oven to 350°F (180°C/Gas 4).

4. Using a colander, drain water from soaked beans and rinse. Place in a blender. Add ¾ cup water, red hot pepper, red bell pepper, ginger and onion.

5. Blend thoroughly and pour mix into a large bowl. Use remaining water to rinse blender. Freshly grind calabash nutmeg or grate nutmeg into mixture, add salt and 1 teaspoon of Zomi. Mix thoroughly with a wooden spoon.

6. After mixing, beat Koose mixture for about 5 minutes with the wooden spoon, then whisk or use an electric mixer at low speed to aerate the mixture for fluffy Koose end results. Traditionally, the hand is used to beat the Koose till it's almost double in quantity. Feel free to do the same.

7. Grab two 12-count mini muffin pans or pans of choice. Silicone baking pans work wonders here. Generously brush the bottoms and sides of each cavity or compartment with vegetable oil. Fill each cavity with about a tablespoon of Koose mix. Repeat for all of the cavities in the muffin pan.

8. Place in oven, let bake for about 30–35 minutes, or until golden brown.

9. Remove from oven, turn pan upside-down on a cooling rack to gently release Koose.

10. Let cool for about 5 minutes and serve these scrumptious bites!

> **Tip 3: Raise the stakes with fresh banana or plantain leaves**
> Use freshly cut banana or plantain leaves to line pan of choice. Rinse and clean the freshly cut leaves, cut to fit size of pan, and lightly brush with oil before filling with Koose mixture.

Pinkaso

For Dough

- 2 cups (10½oz/300g) all-purpose flour
- 1 small (6oz/170g) yellow onion
- 1 Scotch Bonnet (Habanero pepper)
- ¼ tsp salt
- 1 tsp baking powder
- 1 tbsp dry yeast
- 8 tbsp (½ cup/4oz) warm water
- 1 egg

For Frying

- 3 cups (24fl oz/750ml) vegetable oil

For Sprinkling

- 4 tsp sugar

Preparation

1. In a blender, combine onion and Habanero pepper into a smooth blended mix. Pour mix into a large mixing bowl, add egg, and beat with whisk to mix completely.

2. Add warm water, salt, and yeast, and continue to beat. Gradually fold in flour and add baking powder. Gently continue mixing till all ingredients bind together into a soft sticky dough. Resume beating to aerate dough for about 5 minutes.

3. Cover with a damp cloth. Leave in warm place for about 30 minutes to proof dough or until dough is almost twice in size.

Serves: 6 | Prep Time: 45 minutes | Frying Time: 25 minutes

4. Heat oil in a large frying pan over medium-high. To check and confirm oil is hot for frying to begin, cut a small piece of lemon or orange rind and gently drop into the oil. The lemon or orange rind will immediately rise from the bottom of the pan to the top and start browning. Or use a piece of bread, which turns golden in seconds. Pick out rind or bread and discard.

5. The hand is traditionally used to scoop a sizeable amount in the palm while simultaneously creating a hole in the center with the thumb and then gently dropping into the oil.

Alternatively, use a tablespoon or ice cream scoop. Dip in water, scoop some dough, then use a wooden skewer or chopstick to create an opening in the center of each scoop before dropping gently into oil. Adding one scoop at a time, do not overcrowd frying pan.

A doughnut batter dispenser can simplify the process and easily help create the hole and make the dough dropping into the oil a little more seamless as well.

6. Fry for about 7–12 minutes or until all sides are golden brown. Turn Pinkaso pieces at least once during the frying time with a large slotted spoon or wooden skewer.

7. Remove Pinkaso with the slotted spoon into a mesh sieve or mesh strainer for about 5 minutes to drain excess oil. Transfer to a plate or tray lined with kitchen paper or paper towel to continue draining any extra oil.

8. Repeat process till all of the dough is fried.

9. Sprinkle Pinkaso with sugar and enjoy with your favorite porridge or drink.

> **Tip: Omit the egg!**
> Feel free to omit the egg.

Aluguntugui Delight

Serves: 4 | Prep Time: 10 minutes | Blend Time: 5 minutes

The green distinct fruit with dark dots all over its skin, Aluguntugui (pronounced "alu-guun-to-gween"), also called soursop and guanabana in other parts of the world, is a well-known power-packed fruit that does wonders for the body. This healthy pack of nature, in collaboration with others from nature's fruit garden, is here to delight you with a new splashing and refreshing tropical drink. Relax, sip, and enjoy the delightful leap of this tropical drink.

For The Blend

- 3lb (50oz/1.4kg) soft, ripen Aluguntugui (soursop)
- 1½lb (42oz/680g) pineapple, peeled, cut fresh
- 8 oranges
- 2 lemons
- 6 cups (48fl oz/1.5L) water
- pinch of cayenne pepper

Preparation

1. Wash and cut Aluguntugui (soursop) lengthwise into half. Using a spoon, scoop out the pulp and remove seeds.

2. Cut oranges into quarters and remove seeds. Pull and peel each whole orange pulp from skin of the quarters.

3. Combine Aluguntugui (soursop), pineapple, and orange into a blender. Add 5 cups of water and juice of one lemon. Blend completely into a smooth mixture.

4. Pour mix into a pitcher and rinse blender of mixture debris with remaining 1 cup of water. Add rinsed debris to pitcher. Mix and stir.

5. Divide into serving cups. Top with zest of remaining lemon and enjoy!

> **Tip: Green oranges & lemons?**
> Oranges in Ghana are green and yellow in colour. Lemons are also green as compared to other parts of the world.

Sobolo Mango Smoothie

Serves: 6

Prep Time: 20 minutes

Cooking Time: 60 minutes

A smoothie with the DNA of Sobolo written all over it but full of mango's playful side. All Sobolo's benefits plus mango's sweetness to put you in a right mood. It's really not that serious; laugh a little!

For Sobolo
• 5oz (142g) Sobolo (Hibiscus Flowers/Sorrel)

For Boiling Spices
• 8 pods Hwentia (Grains of Selim)
• 10 whole Star Anise
• 1 tsp Wie Din (Esoro Wisa/Black Peppercorns)
• 1½ tsp whole cloves
• 9 cups (72fl oz/2.1L) water

For Cooling
• 4½ cups (34fl oz/1L) iced water

> **Tip : A bit of Tiger Nuts to smoothie blend**
> Add 4oz (113g) fresh Tiger Nuts for a bit more roar.

For The Blend
• 2oz (57g) ginger root, peeled
• 6 cloves garlic
• 6 tbsp Baobab powder
• 1lb (16oz/454g) mango, peeled, chopped fresh
• 2 cups (16fl oz/474ml) water

Preparation

1. In a large pot, add spices to water, cover with lid, and bring to a boil over high heat for 15 minutes.

2. Meanwhile, pour Sobolo on a tray and spend a few minutes or less to carefully pick out anything other than the flowers, such as bits of chaff or any foreign particles. Rinse and add Sobolo to the boiling spices. Stir and continue cooking for 15 more minutes over medium heat.

3. Turn heat off and let sit for 10 minutes. Then, pour mixture through a sieve into a bowl to cool. Pour the iced water into another bowl, place the sieve with cooked spice and Sobolo content in it for 5 minutes.

4. Put ginger, garlic, mango, and baobab powder into a blender. Lift sieve off of ice water bowl, shake off excess liquid, while pressing contents with a spoon. Add liquid into blender. Then add the main liquid from the other bowl and blend into a smoothie.

5. Pour smoothie into serving cups and rinse blender of smoothie debris with remaining 1 cup of water. Add rinsed debris to smoothie and stir. The smoothie is for your vacation!

Rhythm & Beet Smoothie

Serves: 4 | **Prep Time:** 10 minutes | **Blend Time:** 5 minutes

Rhythm & Beet Smoothie is the pick-me-up for those off-beat days. Get your rhythm and beat back on track with this smoothie to realign your day. Don't go off track or off sync; no, not you!

For The Blend

- 2 medium (24oz/680g) beets, peeled, chopped fresh
- ½lb (8oz/227g) pineapple, peeled, cut fresh
- 2 small (6oz/170g) tangerines, seedless, peeled
- 4oz (113g) mango, chopped fresh
- 1oz (28g) ginger root, peeled, cut into chunks
- 2 tbsp Baobab powder
- 3 cups (25fl oz/750ml) water

Preparation

1. Combine ingredients into a blender, add 2¾ cups water and blend into a smoothie.

2. Pour smoothie into serving cups and rinse blender of smoothie debris with remaining ¼ cup water. Add rinsed debris to smoothie and stir.

3. Straw. Drop. It's your smoothie. Treat yourself!

Tip 1: Top with mango!
Top the smoothie with some 2–3 inches mango strips

Tip 2: Get that ginger kick!
Add 1–2oz more of ginger to get that extra ginger kick to the smoothie.

Tip 3: A bit passion fruit to smoothie blend
Add 4oz (113g) fresh passion fruit for a bit more of your passionate side.

Cocoa Plantain

Serves: 25 | Prep Time: 30 minutes | Baking Time: 25 minutes

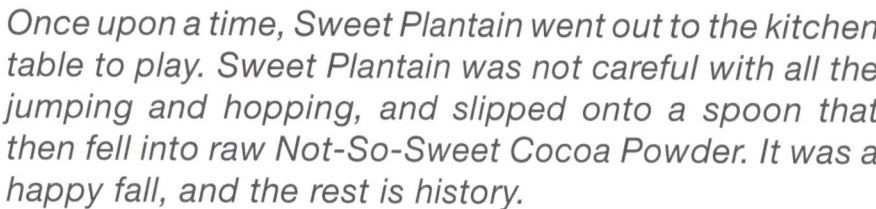

Once upon a time, Sweet Plantain went out to the kitchen table to play. Sweet Plantain was not careful with all the jumping and hopping, and slipped onto a spoon that then fell into raw Not-So-Sweet Cocoa Powder. It was a happy fall, and the rest is history.

Cocoa Plantain is a hybrid between a bread and a pastry. During its initial focus group testing, one anonymous participant said, "It tasted like bread but different." The name Cocoa Plantain really sums up what it is. The raw cocoa bitter side fuses well with the sweet plantain into a bittersweet experience and works well as a base to hold any of your favourite toppings of jams, avocado slices, stews, vegetables, and wherever your imagination can take you. But remember, it's the love between cocoa and plantain that's taking you to new places in your taste and food journey.

For Pastry Mix

- 2 cups (10½oz/300g) flour
- 8 tbsp margarine
- 1 tbsp olive oil
- ¼ tsp salt
- 1 tsp baking powder
- 1 tsp nutmeg
- 8tbsp (½ cup/4oz) iced water

For Cocoa

- 5 tbsp natural cocoa powder

For Plantain Mash

- 2 soft ripened plantains
- 1 tbsp water

For Brushing Top

- 1 tsp margarine

Preparation

1. Make pastry by combining flour, salt, nutmeg, and baking powder in a food processor. Pulse on and off for a few seconds to mix completely. Add margarine and olive oil. Pulse on and off for about 5 minutes to mix to a texture that leaves tiny margarine bits about the size of a grain of corn.

Alternatively, a pastry blender or your fingers can be used in the absence of a food processor to blend in and mix margarine, olive oil and dry ingredients. This method might require an additional 5–8 minutes for thorough mix.

2. Set aside 4 tablespoons of the pastry mix for rolling pastry. Divide the remaining pastry into two parts and place in two separate bowls with covers.

3. Add the cocoa powder to first part and slowly add 4 tablespoons of iced water in small amounts as you keep pulsing on and off in food processor or mixing with your fingers until dough comes together and begins to stick. Form a dough ball. Place dough ball in bowl, cover and refrigerate in freezer for at least 10 minutes or chill in fridge overnight.

4. Add remaining 4 tablespoons of water to the second part pastry mix. Form a second dough ball. Place the second dough ball in bowl, cover and refrigerate as well in freezer for at least 10 minutes or chill in fridge overnight.

5. Prep a baking sheet by lightly greasing it. Preheat oven to 450°F (230°C/Gas 8).

6. Cut plantain skin lengthwise and scrape all of the mushy soft plantain out into a mortar with a spoon. Use the pestle to crush, mash and mix plantains, and one tablespoon of water into a lump-free mixture or use the earthenware grinding bowl and its wooden masher.

Alternatively, a food processor can be used to mash the plantains into a lump-free plantain mixture by pulsing on and off for about a minute or two, or use a potato ricer mash.

7. Grab the two dough balls from the freezer. Dust work surface with pastry mix. Gently shape both dough balls into short ropes 8-inches (20 cm). With the two short dough ropes, press together, twist and braid into one form.

8. Using a rolling pin, roll out the combined dough to a rectangle about 1/8inch (3mm) in thickness. Then pour and evenly spread the mashed plantain onto rolled-out pastry dough. Lift and carefully roll up dough firmly from one of the longer edges into a ready-to-bake Cocoa Plantain. Pinch and close ends.

9. Lift and place on baking sheet. Using a fork or a table knife, punch deep holes on top to serve as air pockets. Melt the teaspoon of margarine and brush before placing in the oven. The margarine will give it a baked golden shine.

10. Place in oven for 5 minutes and then reduce heat to 375°F (190°C/Gas 5). Let bake for about 20–25 minutes. Rotate tray at least once during baking time for even baking on all sides. Let bake until tops are golden brown. Remove and place Cocoa Plantain on a cooling rack.

11. Let cool for 10 minutes and cut the roll into 20 slices or desired thickness to serve, or top with your favorite combination of stews, meats, or vegetables.

Tip: Top it your own style
Top with a teaspoon of tomato stew and a slice of avocado or Red Red or a tuna salad or meat of choice.

ALL YOU CAN PLANTAIN & MORE

1 2 3 4 5 6 7

Plantain is the cousin of banana but has a denser texture. Plantains are not eaten raw like bananas but require cooking before consumption. Plantains can be utilized in different recipes throughout the ripening stages. From the time it's fresh and vibrant green to the point where the skin is completely black and looks absolutely dead, there's a Tropical Ghana recipe to maximize this very special ingredient.

Plantains become ripe when the colour changes from green to yellow. And when ripe, it is naturally sweet in the recipe it is used in. Ripe plantains become caramelized when fried, with the edges building a tasty crust.

1 - Good for Plantain Fufu, Boiled as Ampesi, Tasty Plantain Chips

2 - Boiled and enjoyed with stews

3 - Perfect for Plantain Otɔ/Etɔ (Otor)

4 - Ideal for Roasted Plantains

5 - Frying for Red Red, Yoo Kɛ Gari, plus Ginger Oven Plantains

6 - Frying for Kelewele

7 - That sweet spot very ripened for Tatale (Plantain Pancakes) and Ablongo (Plantain Cakes)

The Ghana Plantain Cuts

Ghana Kofi Brokeman Plantain Cut

Ghana Kofi Brokeman Plantain Cut is popular for selling roasted plantains on the streets of Ghana. At about an angle of 45°, diagonally slice the plantains across the length. Depending on the length, each plantain can yield about two or three pieces.

Universal Ghana Plantain Cut

Universal Ghana Plantain Cut is achieved when you cut the plantain along its length into two pieces. This is also another cut for roasting.

Half-A-Dozen Universal Ghana Plantain Cut

The Half-A-Dozen Universal Ghana Plantain Cut is achieved when you cut the plantain across the length into three equal parts. Then cut each of the three parts along its length, creating six pieces.

Ghana Plantain Slice (Red Red Cut)

Ghana Plantain Slice, aka Red Red Cut, is for enjoying the dish Red Red. Diagonally slice the plantains across the length into sizes of about ¼-inch (6mm) in thickness. The slice presents a unique "eat-ready" shape and to dip and scoop the Red Red to enjoy.

Ghana Kelewele Cut

Ghana Kelewele Cut is a unique and well-known style on the streets of Accra. Peel plantains and slice in half lengthwise. Cut ½-inch (12mm) thick pieces at a slight diagonal across the length of each halved plantain. Add Kelewele spice and a bit of salt, then thoroughly mix until plantain pieces are well coated with the spice.

Forever Kelewele Ghana Cut

Forever Kelewele Ghana Cut is a stylized Kelewele Cut. Peel plantains and slice in half lengthwise. Cut ½-inch (12mm) thick pieces across each halved plantain.

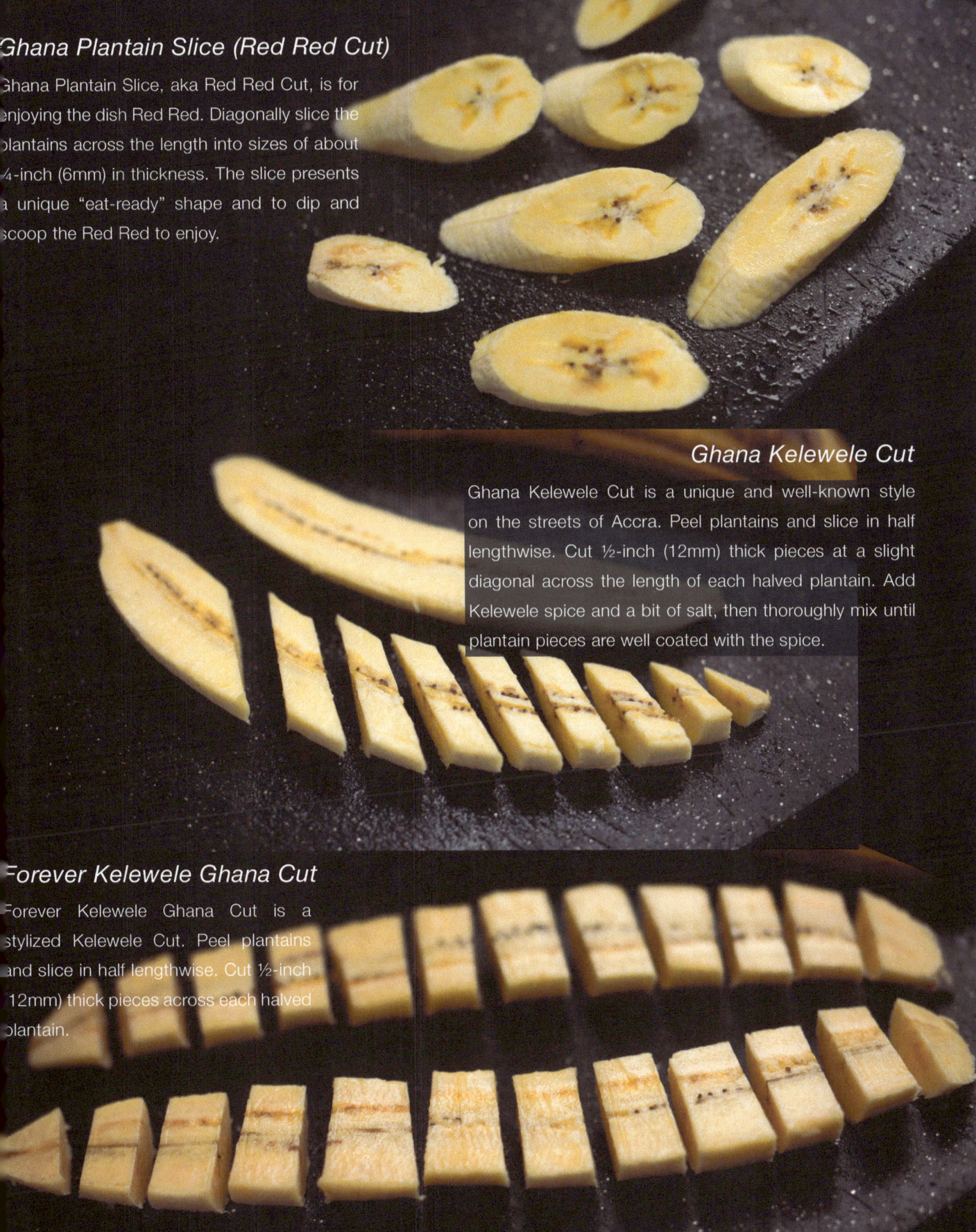

Kofi Brokeman/Roasted Plantains

Serves: 6 | **Prep Time:** 5 minutes | **Roasting Time:** 20 minutes

Kofi Brokeman! Yes, that's the street name for Roasted Plantains. Somehow, some way, this meal got the name Kofi Brokeman because it's believed to be so affordable that a person who is broke with some coins in his or her pocket can afford it and have a simple, decent meal when paired with roasted Ghana groundnuts.

Roasted Plantains are very simple and wholesome, and a snack that can easily be found on the streets of Ghana. It's normally charcoal-grilled over low heat by Ghanaian women and complemented with Ghana's tasty, roasted groundnuts.

Try it! You will realize that it's packed with goodness available to all and not only for a person who is a little broke. Roasted plantains with groundnuts — a simple affordable meal for any family on a budget. These days, the masses keep voicing out Kofi Brokeman is becoming Kofi Richman because of the rising price on the streets. It's time to make your own, or?

For Roasting
- 3 ripe plantains (yellow), hard, j

For Nuts
- 6 tbsp roasted groundnuts (peanuts) or roasted cashews or your favorite nuts

> **Tip: Bring the kids on board with more excitement!**
> Get the kids on board to help spread each grilled plantain with groundnut paste (peanut butter), then top with slices of red, yellow, and green bell peppers.

Preparation

1. Preheat grill or turn the broiler of your cooking unit on. Or go authentic and fire your charcoal grill.

2. On a chopping board, cut the ends of the plantains off with a table knife. Then gently cut the skin along the length of each plantain and peel the skin off.

3. Cut the plantain along its length into two parts for the Universal Ghana cut. Or cut across the length into three equal parts. Then cut each of the three parts along its length into two, creating six pieces from each plantain for the Half-A-Dozen Universal Ghana plantain cut.

Alternatively, go simple and authentic by using the popular street cut – the Ghana Kofi Brokeman Plantain Cut.

At about an angle of 45°, diagonally slice the plantains across the length to ¾-inch (18mm) thick pieces. Each plantain yields about 2–3 pieces.

4. Reduce grill to medium low and place plantains on the grill or on a broiler pan covered with aluminum foil. Let grill or broil for about 7–10 minutes on each side, checking occasionally until light brown. Then flip the plantains pieces to grill the opposite sides.

5. As plantains grill gently, grab a plate and get the nuts ready.

6. Serve plantains right off the grill, hot with the roasted nuts of your choice. It's your Kofi Brokeman day!

Boiled Plantains

Serves: 3
Prep Time: 5 minutes
Cooking Time: 20 minutes

Boiling unripe plantains (green) or ripe plantains (yellow) goes well with stews or soups. Also, they can be added to form part of another recipe to churn out a tasty new dish.

For Cooking Plantain

• 5 partially ripe plantains
• 4 cups (36oz/1L) water
• 1 tsp salt

Preparation

1. Peel and place plantains in a large cooking pot, add water, and bring to boil over medium-high heat for about 20–25 minutes. If plantains are large, cut them into quarters to boil.

2. Check plantains for tenderness with a fork. If fork slides easily into the plantain, it's cooked – similar to how one cooks potatoes. Drain water. Plantains are ready to be enjoyed with stew or soup or in another recipe.

Kelewele

Serves: 6 | **Prep Time:** 10 minutes | **Frying Time:** 25 minutes

The night is young, and the air is filled with the uniquely combined aroma of ginger, cloves, plantains, and more, that calls your name. Say no more! If you know, you know. Kelewele is an evening delicacy that appears when the sun gradually starts going down to rest and street vendors happily help put smiles on faces.

The street champs of this dish always have people in a queue patiently waiting for their turn to get some of this hot goodness to lighten their evening. There's no slacking while you wait in line because it's easy for a person to order for a whole family, which will lead you to wait for the next batch or the one after. But the wait is really worth it.

In the '90s, Kelewele spots in town presented the perfect first affordable budget outing for young men who were on a mission to win a lady's heart. And should a young man manage to land a borrowed car from an uncle or a relative, the car bonnet served as the perfect table to enjoy the Kelewele while speaking his heart out to the lady. Kelewele draws crowds, and when it appears on any buffet table at a party, it is more than likely to vanish first. Get going and get your Kelewele off to a good start!

For Plantain

- 5 soft ripened plantains
- ½ tsp salt

For Frying

- 6 cups (48oz/1.5L) vegetable oil

For Kelewele Spice

- 1 ring slice of yellow onion (1oz/28g)
- 3 cloves garlic
- 5oz (142g) ginger root, peeled, sliced
- 8 whole cloves (1½ tsp ground cloves)
- 5 tsp chili pepper/cayenne powder
- 6 tbsp water

Tip 1: Groundnuts to enjoy
Enjoy the Kelewele with some roasted Ghana Groundnuts.

Tip 2: For less-sweet Kelewele
Use plantains that just turned ripe yellow and are not soft

Tip 3: If using ground cloves, add last
Ground cloves have a tendency to make any spice in their path turn dark on contact. If using ground or powdered cloves, add them last after plantains are mixed with spice.

Preparation

1. In a blender or food processor, blend onion, ginger, garlic, cloves and 3 tablespoons of water. Pour blended spice into bowl. Rinse blender or food processer with remaining water and add to blended spice. Add cayenne pepper powder and mix completely into spice.

Alternatively, and as done traditionally, the onion, ginger, garlic and cloves can be ground in a Ghanaian earthenware grinding bowl (Asanka) with a wooden masher. Add cayenne pepper right into it and mix with the wooden masher. Save some spice in a bowl with lid for later use. Plantain pieces can be tossed right into the Ghanaian earthenware grinding bowl.

2. Using the Ghana Kelewele Cut, peel plantains and slice in half lengthwise. Cut ½-inch (12mm) thick pieces at a slight diagonal across the length of each halved plantain. Salt plantain pieces. Add spice and mix thoroughly until plantain pieces are well-coated.

3. Heat oil in a large deep-frying pan over medium-high. To check and confirm oil is hot to fry, cut a small piece of orange rind and gently drop in oil. The orange rind will immediately rise from the bottom of pan to the top and start browning. Or use a piece of bread, which turns golden in seconds. Pick out orange rind or bread and discard.

4. Using a large slotted spoon, place plantain pieces in oil gently. Deep-fry plantains in 2–3 batches, making sure not to overcrowd the frying pan. Fry for about 12–15 minutes or until all sides are golden brown and done.

5. Meanwhile, use a wooden skewer to gently stir the plantain pieces right after they are placed in the oil. Stirring helps separate the pieces a bit and give each plantain piece a little room to create that individual caramelized crusted exterior. Stir at least twice during the frying time for best results.

6. Remove Kelewele with the large slotted spoon into a mesh sieve or mesh strainer for about 5 minutes to drain excess oil. Transfer to plate lined with kitchen paper or paper towel to continue to drain.

7. Repeat process till all plantain pieces are fried.

8. Kelewele is ready to be enjoyed hot as is or with groundnuts.

Ginger Oven Plantains

Serves: 6 | **Prep Time:** 10 minutes | **Baking Time:** 30 minutes

For the days when the Kelewele feeling is there but no heavy lifting is on the horizon for you. A milder baked grandchild version adapted from the original that keeps your hands a bit freer. Cut, ginger, and oven. Read a book till it's ready.

For Plantain

- 5 ripe plantains
- ¼ tsp salt
- 3 tbsp olive oil (vegetable oil)

For Ginger Blend

- 4oz (113g) ginger root, peeled, sliced
- 6 tbsp water

Optional

- ¾ tsp cayenne pepper

Tip 1: Optional Cayenne
Sprinkle ¾ teaspoon cayenne pepper on plantain pieces before placing in oven.

Tip 2: Try with Sweet Potatoes
Try the ginger blend with sweet potatoes for a Ginger Oven Sweet Potatoes.

Preparation

1. Preheat oven to 450°F (230°C/Gas 8).

2. In a blender or food processor, blend ginger and 4 tablespoons of water. Pour blended spice into bowl. Rinse blender or food processer with remaining water and add to blended spice.

Alternatively, and as done traditionally, the ginger can be ground in a Ghanaian earthenware grinding bowl (Asanka) with a wooden masher. Plantain pieces can be tossed right into the Ghanaian earthenware grinding bowl.

3. Using the Ghana Forever Kelewele Cut, peel plantains and slice in half lengthwise. Cut ½-inch (12mm) thick pieces across the length of each halved plantain. Salt plantain pieces. Using a spoon, add as much ginger blend to generously coat plantain pieces. Save any remaining spice.

4. Drizzle with the olive oil and mix completely for all pieces to be coated. Distribute onto 2 lightly greased baking trays and spread pieces evenly on the trays.

5. Place in oven and let bake. After 5 minutes, reduce heat to 400°F (200°C/Gas 6). Let continue baking for another 25–30 minutes, or until golden brown and done.

Plantain Otɔ/Plantain Etɔ

Serves: 6 | **Prep Time:** 10 minutes | **Cooking Time:** 25 minutes

Plantain Otɔ/Etɔ (Otor) is a mash of boiled plantains mixed with palm oil, topped with boiled eggs. All the action happens in an Asanka when the plantain comes right off the fire and the heat helps melt the palm oil into it. Here's a version for all champions.

For Cooking Plantain

- 6 partially ripe plantains
- 4½ cups (36oz/1L) water
- 1½ tsp salt

For Boiling Eggs

- 6 eggs
- 3 cups (25fl oz/750ml) water
- 1 tsp salt

For Zomi Stew

- 3½ tbsp Zomi (spiced palm oil)
- 1 medium (6oz/170g) tomato, blended
- 1 small yellow onion (4oz/113g), finely chopped
- ½ Scotch Bonnet (Habanero) pepper, finely chopped
- 1 clove of garlic, finely chopped
- ½ tsp minced ginger
- 1 tsp dried shrimp powder
- ½ tsp salt

Preparation

1. Peel and cut each plantain into three pieces across the length. Place in a large cooking pot, add water, and bring to boil over medium-high heat for about 20–25 minutes.

2. Place eggs into another cooking pot, add water, and let boil over medium heat for 15 minutes. Remove eggs into a bowl of tap water to cool.

3. Meanwhile, warm palm oil in a saucepan over medium heat. Add Scotch Bonnet, red onion, ginger, garlic and salt. Stir continuously for about 5–8 minutes.

4. Add tomatoes and mix completely. Cover saucepan with lid and let cook for about 5 minutes.

5. Add dried shrimp powder and stir continuously for 2 minutes.

6. Reduce heat to low and simmer for 5 minutes uncovered.

7. Check plantains for tenderness with a fork. If fork slides easily into the plantain, it's cooked – similar to how one cooks potatoes. Drain water and mash plantains hot. Plantain is mashed traditionally in the clay grinding bowl, Asanka, with a wooden grinder. If available, use an Asanka.

8. Add Zomi Stew into mashed plantains and mix through and through. Peel eggs, place whole or cut in half or quartered. Garnish Plantain Otor with eggs and serve.

Ablongo/Ofam/Plantain Cakes

Serves: 6 | **Prep Time:** 15 minutes | **Baking Time:** 25 minutes

For Plantain Cake Mix

- 5 extremely soft, over-ripened plantains
- 4 tbsp roasted corn flour, corn meal, millet flour, or brown rice flour
- 2 tbsp ginger, freshly minced or 1 tbsp ginger powder
- ½ tsp crushed red pepper (¼ tsp cayenne pepper)
- 5 tsp spiced palm oil (Zomi)
- pinch of salt
- 8 tbsp (4fl oz/125ml) water

Preparation

1. Preheat oven to 350°F (180°C/ Gas 4).

2. Grab a wooden mortar and pestle to use. Traditionally, a mortar and pestle or a Ghanaian earthenware grinding bowl (Asanka) with wood masher are used and mix plantains.

3. Cut plantain skin lengthwise and scrape all of the mushy soft plantain out into the mortar with a spoon. Use the pestle to crush, mash and mix plantains into a lump free mixture or use the earthenware grinding bowl with wood masher.

Alternatively, a food processor can be used to mash the plantains into a lump-free plantain mixture.

4. Pour plantain mix into a bowl. Use water to rinse the mortar or food processor. Add ginger, crushed red pepper, palm oil and salt. Mix thoroughly. Gently fold in flour of choice and mix completely. If using the Ghanaian earthenware grinding bowl to crush and mash the plantains, continue mixing there.

5. Grab a 12-count mini muffin pan or pan of choice. Generously brush the bottoms and sides of each cavity or compartment with vegetable oil. Fill each cavity with about a tablespoon of the plantain mix. Repeat for all of the cavities or compartments in the muffin pan.

6. Place in oven and bake for about 25–30 minutes, or until baked and golden brown. Remove from oven and let caramelized plantain solidify for about 5 minutes. Turn pan upside-down on a cooling rack to gently release plantain cakes.

Tip 1: Other flour
Corn flour, breadcrumbs, or your favorite flour can be used.

Tip 2: Is it baked?
A toothpick can be inserted into the plantain cake to check if baked. If completely baked, the toothpick will come out clean without wet plantain bits.

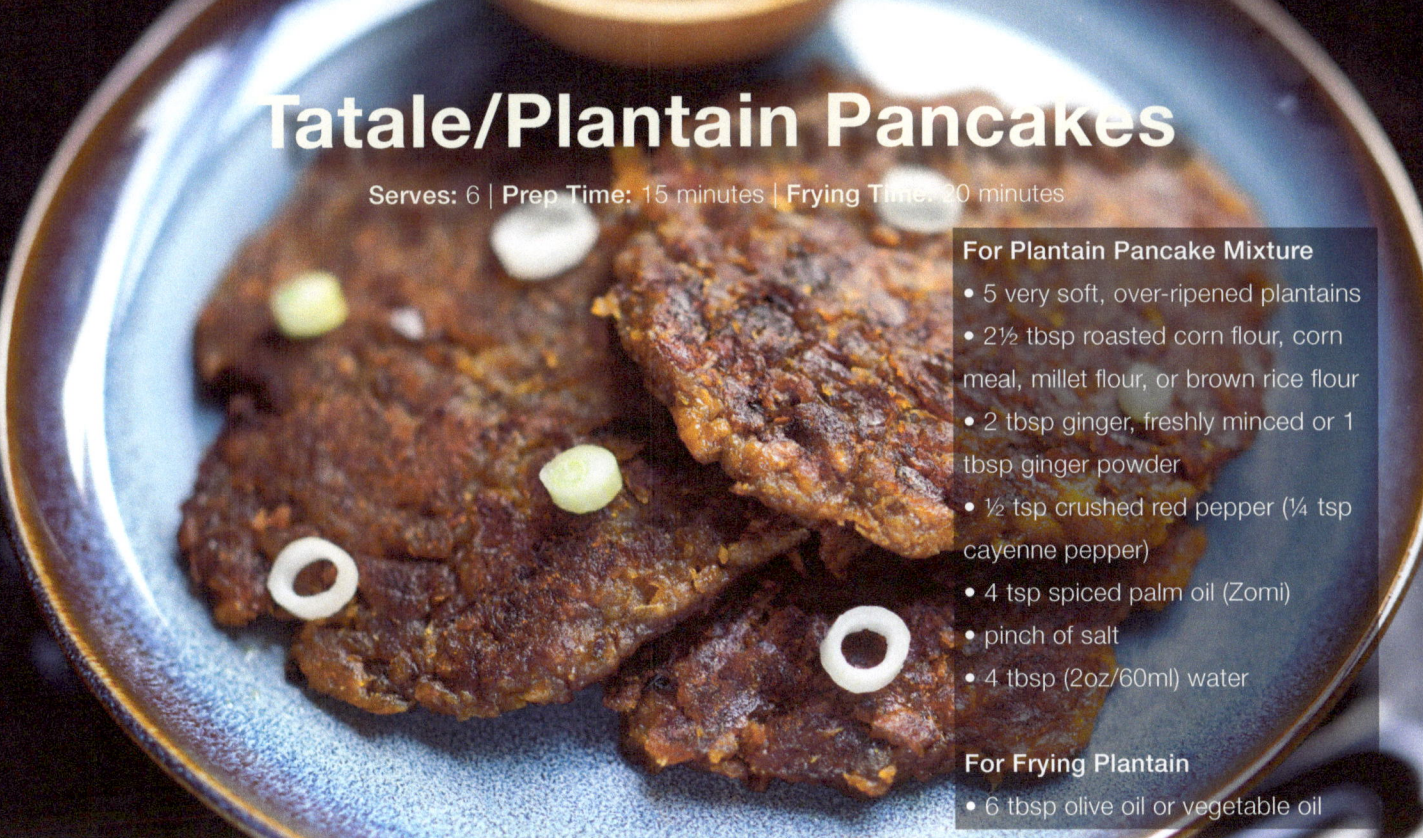

Tatale/Plantain Pancakes

Serves: 6 | Prep Time: 15 minutes | Frying Time: 20 minutes

For Plantain Pancake Mixture
- 5 very soft, over-ripened plantains
- 2½ tbsp roasted corn flour, corn meal, millet flour, or brown rice flour
- 2 tbsp ginger, freshly minced or 1 tbsp ginger powder
- ½ tsp crushed red pepper (¼ tsp cayenne pepper)
- 4 tsp spiced palm oil (Zomi)
- pinch of salt
- 4 tbsp (2oz/60ml) water

For Frying Plantain
- 6 tbsp olive oil or vegetable oil

Preparation

1. Grab a wooden mortar and pestle to use. Traditionally, a mortar and pestle or a Ghanaian earthenware grinding bowl (Asanka) with wood masher is used to mix plantains.

2. Cut plantain skin lengthwise and scrape all the mushy soft plantain out into the mortar with a spoon. Use the pestle to crush, mash and mix plantains into a lump-free mixture or use the earthenware grinding bowl with a wooden masher.

Alternatively, a food processor can be used to mash the plantains into a lump-free plantain mixture by pulsing on and off for about a minute or two.

3. Pour plantain mix into a bowl. Use water to rinse the mortar or food processor. Add ginger, crushed red pepper, palm oil and salt. Mix thoroughly. Gently fold in flour of choice and mix completely. If using the Ghanaian earthenware grinding bowl to crush and mash the plantains, continue mixing there.

4. Grab a nonstick skillet or frying pan and heat a teaspoon of cooking oil over medium heat. Add 2–3 tablespoons of the plantain mix into the skillet depending on skillet size. Gently shake and swivel the skillet around for the mixture to evenly cover enough surface area.

5. Let gently fry for about 5 minutes or until mixture solidifies and golden brown. With a turner, gently turn or flip to cook the other side in the same manner until golden brown.

6. Toss on a plate. Repeat process until all of the mixture is cooked into Tatale.

7. Enjoy the Tatale hot with Aboboi or cooked Bambara Beans, or with your favourite nuts, or as is without any side.

Tip 2: Other flour
Corn flour, breadcrumbs, or your favorite flour can be used.

Tip 1: Just add Aboboi
Tatale goes best with Aboboi.

PLANTAINS' FRIENDSHIP WITH BEANS

Beans in Ghana are about enjoyment on another level. Different dishes feature different kinds of beans that keeps adding more and more smiles to any day. Most of these recipes dance well when fried ripe plantains are added as a complement to the dish.

The beans category in Ghana also presents some of the most delicious vegetarian dishes. The most popular dish is Yoo Ke Gari. From Aboboi and Tatale to Red Red and Waakye, every Ghanaian has a beans favourite. And if you are new to the scene, you will soon discover your number one bean dish.

Aboboi

Serves: 8

Prep Time: 4 hours or overnight

Cooking Time: 60 minutes

For Soaking Beans
• 2 cups (16oz/454g) Bambara beans (African yellow beans)
• 4 cups (32fl oz/1L) water

For Cooking Aboboi
• 2 dry whole red hot peppers (dry whole cayenne)
• 1 small yellow onion (2oz/57g)
• 1¼ tsp salt
• 2 grape tomatoes
• 6 cups (48fl oz/1.5L) boiling water

Preparation

1. Pour beans on a tray and spend about 5 minutes or less to carefully pick out anything other than the beans, such as bits of chaff, small stones or particles.

2. Rinse beans with water and use a colander to drain excess water. Place rinsed beans in a large cooking pot and add 4 cups of water. Cover with lid and leave overnight or for 4 hours for beans to absorb water.

3. With a colander, drain water from soaked beans and rinse. Add 6 cups of boiling water. Add salt, partially cover with lid, and let beans boil for about 15 minutes over high heat, stirring occasionally.

4. Reduce heat to medium, add pepper, onion and grape tomatoes. Partially cover with lid and continue cooking for 20 minutes.

5. Pick out the pepper, onion and grape tomatoes into a blender or food processor. Add 3 tablespoons of Bambara beans with liquid from cooking pot and blend completely. Pour blended mix into the boiling beans and mix thoroughly. The blended mix acts as thickener. Add some spice as well.

6. Let simmer for another 20 minutes or until almost all of the liquid is almost absorbed.

7. Grab a plate and scoop some Aboboi onto it. Sprinkle with a teaspoon of sugar or serve as is. Add some Tatale (Plantain Pancakes) and enjoy the dish steaming hot!

Yoo Kε Gari

Yoo Kε Gari is the go-to meal for most people as it can carry anyone far into their daily routine at an affordable price tag. It's the number one complete vegetarian meal for the average Ghanaian. Basically, it's cooked beans topped with Zomi (spiced palm oil) with Gari. It moves slightly up the affordable category when fried plantain are added. Fried plantains make it more enjoyable.

Yoo means beans in the Ga language, so beans and Gari. Some like to sprinkle a little Gari while others like more Gari. Masons have even popularized the way the Gari mixture ratio is preferred, naming it "concrete" in reference to their line of work, to attain the right mixture for a solid daily body foundation.

Lovers of this meal will occasionally buy the beans, add fresh ground pepper, and eat it with boiled yam or steamed rice. Bean eateries that sell this meal have evolved to meet the growing additional needs such as boiled eggs.

In recent times, a newer nickname has emerged with no clear meaning. A school of thought claim Gari, Oil, Beans, Egg is GOBE but it completely sounds out of place for this timeless classic from generations past. No! No more of this corruption! It starts with beans. It will always be Yoo kε Gari forever.

Serves: 6
Prep Time: 4 hours or overnight
Cooking Time: 45 minutes

For Cooking Beans

• 2 cups (16oz/454g) black eye beans
• 4 cups (32fl oz/1L) water
• 6 cups (48fl oz/1.5L) boiling water
• 2 tsp salt

For Frying Plantain

• 6 soft ripe plantains
• 3 cups (24fl oz/750ml) vegetable oil

Beans are enjoyed with Gari.

Tip 1: Top with Zomi-Under
Add the highly coveted tasty debris that settles at the bottom of Zomi, the coveted Zomi-Under, to elevate the taste.

Preparation

1. Pour beans on a tray and spend about 5 minutes or less to carefully pick out anything other than the beans, such as bits of chaff, small stones, or particles.

2. Rinse beans with water and use a colander to drain excess water. Place rinsed beans in a large cooking pot and add 4 cups of water. Cover with lid and leave overnight or for 4 hours for beans to absorb water.

3. Using a colander, drain water from soaked beans and rinse. Add 6 cups of boiling water and salt. Let beans boil for about 25 minutes on high, stirring occasionally. Skim off foam that rises to the top as beans cook.

4. Reduce heat to low, partially cover with lid, and allow beans to simmer till a little liquid remains.

5. Meanwhile, peel the plantains. Use the Ghana Red Red plantain cut by diagonally slicing the plantains across the length into sizes of about ¼-inch (6mm) in thickness.

6. Heat oil in frying pan over medium-high heat. To check and confirm oil is hot to start frying, gently drop a small piece of orange rind in the oil with a spoon. The orange rind will immediately rise from the bottom of the pan to the top and start browning. Or use a piece of bread, which will turn golden in seconds. Pick out orange rind or piece of bread and discard.

7. Deep-fry plantain slices for about 15–20 minutes over medium heat until plantain slices are golden brown on all sides. Flip or turn plantain slices at least once during frying to get all sides golden brown.

8. Using a slotted spoon, remove plantain slices, and place into a mesh sieve or mesh strainer for about 5 minutes to drain excess oil. Then place on paper towel or kitchen paper to continue to drain excess oil.

9. Serve the beans with Zomi, Zomi-Under, and the fried plantains plus Gari. Enjoy the power pack that will keep you well-grounded for the day.

Tip 2: Check beans for "extras" or anything foreign
It's important to carefully examine beans when in use in any recipe to pick out anything other than the beans, such as bits of chaff, small stones, or particles. Rinse and you are on your way to making a great bean recipe.

Red Red

Serves: 6 | Prep Time: 4 hours or overnight | Cooking Time: 70 minutes

Why paint the town red when Red Red can be enjoyed anytime? Red Red is the established nickname given to Ghana's Black Eye Beans Stew that is eaten with fried plantains.

Red Red takes its name from the colour of the palm oil used in cooking the stew, and also from the fried plantain, which has hints of red when very ripe and fried.

A stewed version of Yoo Kε Gari and well-known boarding school favourite, Red Red is a complete vegetarian meal loved by all. It's enjoyed all over Ghana and one can easily spot groups of people having hearty chats while doing justice to this meal.

Like Yoo Kε Gari, Red Red is topped with Gari, but the stew can also be eaten with boiled Ghana Yam (West African Yam), cocoyam, cooked rice and more, or enjoyed as a stew like any other Ghanaian stew.

For Cooking Beans
• 2 cups (16oz/454g) black eye beans
• 4 cups (32fl oz/1L) water
• 6 cups (48fl oz/1.5L) boiling water
• 2 tsp salt

For Frying Plantain
• 6 soft ripe plantains
• 3 cups (24fl oz/750ml) vegetable oil

For Tomato Stew
• 8 tbsp (4fl oz/125ml) palm oil
• 8 medium tomatoes (2lbs/1kg)
• 1 large red onion (10oz/284g), finely chopped
• 1 Scotch Bonnet (Habanero), pepper finely chopped
• 4 cloves garlic, finely chopped
• 2 tsp ginger, freshly minced
• 2 tsp salt
• 2 tsp tomato puree (or paste)

Preparation

1. Pour beans on a tray and spend about 5 minutes or less to carefully pick out anything other than the beans such as bits of chaff, small stones or particles.

2. Rinse beans with water and use a colander to drain excess water. Place rinsed beans in a large cooking pot and add 4 cups of water. Cover with lid and leave overnight or for 4 hours for beans to absorb water.

3. Using a colander, drain water from soaked beans and rinse. Add 6 cups of boiling water and salt. Let beans boil for about 25 minutes over high heat, stirring occasionally. Skim off foam that rises to the top as beans cook.

4. Reduce heat to low, partially cover with lid, and allow beans to simmer till a little liquid remains.

5. Meanwhile, combine palm oil, red onion, garlic, ginger, Scotch Bonnet pepper and salt in saucepan, over high heat for about 5–7 minutes, stirring continuously.

6. Add tomato puree to sizzling red onion mix when onion bits soften and begin to turn golden brown on the edges. Continue stirring for about 2 minutes, mixing in puree.

7. Cut tomatoes into quarters and blend in a food processor or blender. Add blended tomatoes and mix completely. Cover saucepan with lid and let cook.

8. After 10 minutes, reduce heat to medium. Tip lid slightly so saucepan is partly covered to allow some steam to escape. Let stew continue to cook for 15 minutes, stirring occasionally.

9. Reduce heat to low, add beans to tomato stew, and mix completely. Let simmer for another 5–10 minutes.

10. As the bean stew cooks, peel the plantains. Use the Ghana Red Red plantain cut by diagonally slicing the plantains across the length into ¼-inch pieces.

11. Heat oil in frying pan over medium-high heat. To check and confirm oil is hot to start frying, gently drop a small piece of orange rind in the oil with a spoon. The orange rind will immediately rise from the bottom of the pan to the top and start browning. Or use a piece of bread, which will turn golden in seconds. Pick out orange rind or piece of bread and discard.

12. Deep-fry plantain slices for about 15–20 minutes over medium heat, until plantain slices are golden brown on all sides. Flip or turn plantain slices at least once during frying to get all sides golden brown.

13. Using a slotted spoon, remove plantain slices and place into a mesh sieve or mesh strainer for about 5 minutes to drain excess oil. Then place on paper towel or kitchen paper to continue to drain excess oil.

14. Serve the stew with the fried plantains and Gari. Enjoy Red Red, Tropical Ghana style.

Tip 1: Check beans for "extras"

It's important to carefully examine beans when in use in any recipe to pick out anything other than the beans, such as bits of chaff, small stones or particles. Rinse and you are on your way to making a great bean recipe.

Tip 2: Some toppings maybe?

Feel free to add some smoked tuna pieces and chopped scallions or green onions.

Waakye

Serves: 5

Prep Time: 4 hours or overnight

Cooking Time: 65 minutes

Waakye (pronounced "waa-chay") is Ghana's own very special meal of rice and beans that consistently keeps heads turning in every direction when that unique authentic aroma fills the air. It ignites only smiles and happiness; the rest is patience to have your hot plate for further action.

From northern Ghana and widely available across the length and breadth of the country, Waakye is traditionally sold in the leaves of the Sweet Prayer plant (Katemfe plant). Waakye gets sweeter in the leaf wrap. When unwrapped, the added aroma and sweetness from the leaf takes the meal to a very special place.

Waakye is typically served with Gari, black Shitɔ, Wele, Waakye stew, fish or meats, boiled egg, Taalia (spaghetti dipped in oil of Waakye stew), fried plantains and additions of chopped lettuce, cabbage, onion, and carrot mix or similar. The selection is yours to decide. And the action is solely in your hands.

For Soaking Beans

• 2 cups (16oz/454g) black eye beans

• 4 cups (32fl oz/1L) water

78

For Waakye Stew
• Follow on page 142

For Cooking Waakye

• 1½ cups (12oz/340g) long-grain rice
• 5 cups (41oz/1.2L) boiling water
• 5 tsp salt
• 2 pieces Waakye colour leaf (dried red sorghum stalk), cleaned, trimmed to 3 inches

> **Tip: Check beans for "extras" or anything foreign**
>
> It's important to carefully examine beans when in use in any recipe to pick out anything other than the beans, such as bits of chaff, small stones or particles. Rinse and you are on your way to making a great bean recipe.

Preparation

1. Pour beans on a tray and spend about 5 minutes or less to carefully pick out anything other than the beans, such as bits of chaff, small stones or particles.

2. Rinse beans with water and use a colander to drain excess water. Place rinsed beans in a large cooking pot and add 4 cups of water. Cover and leave overnight or for at least 4 hours for beans to absorb the water.

3. Using a colander, drain water from soaked beans and rinse. Add 5 cups of boiling water and salt. Rinse and add trimmed Waakye leaf. Let beans boil for about 25 minutes over high heat, stirring occasionally.

4. Wash and add rice to boiling beans. Stir rice and beans thoroughly for a uniform mix. Let it boil for another 7–10 minutes or until almost all of the liquid is absorbed. Reduce the heat to the lowest temperature and cover with lid.

5. After 10 minutes, give rice and beans a last stir. Replace lid and let cook for another 10–15 minutes.

6. Turn heat off and let stand for 5 minutes without opening the pot. Serve the Waakye with preferred meats, Waakye Stew and other sides that celebrate its legendary status.

79

LAND, WATER, SEA & THE FISHING ESTATE

Blessed with the Atlantic Ocean, Volta Lake, Lake Bosomtwi, River Ankobra and many freshwater bodies, Ghana abounds in fresh fish and much more such as shrimp, octopus, and crabs. Fried fish is the most common way of finding ready-to-eat fish.

However, the fish varieties are numerous – Cassava Croaker, Red Fish (Snapper), Herrings, Whitting, Grouper, Sole, Tilapia, Mackerel, Tuna, Atlantic Bumper, Catfish, and many more. Tilapia and Mackerel tend to lead the pack on the grilled fish scene.

Grilled Tilapia

Serves: 6

Marinade & Prep Time: 15 minutes

Cooking Time: 25 minutes

Tilapia is here and that's it! Get your charcoal grill fired and get going with some Tilapia on fire. Marinade Tilapia in the spice before grilling; and the longer, the better.

For Fish
- 2 large whole Tilapia, scaled, gutted, cleaned
- 1¾ tsp salt

For Grilling
- 2 tbsp vegetable oil

For Tilapia Spice
- 1 red onion (4oz/113g), peeled
- 6oz (170g) ginger root, peeled
- 6 cloves garlic
- 20 Kpakpo Shitɔ (12 Scotch Bonnet/7 Habanero) pepper
- 2 pods Hwentia (Grains of Selim) or ¾ tsp peppercorn

> **Tip: Aromatic lime note end**
> End on an aromatic lime note with some light lime zest topping.

Preparation

1. Preheat grill or turn on the broiler of your cooking unit.

2. On a chopping board, score fish on both sides or gently cut three diagonal slashes on each side of the fish or shallow cuts, just shy of reaching the bone. And then salt the fish.

3. Combine the Tilapia spice ingredients in a blender or food processor into paste.

Alternatively, the earthenware grinding bowl with its wooden masher can be used to combine the spice ingredients into a paste.

4. Using your fingers, fill the slashes or cavities on skin first with the spice. Then coat inside and the rest of the fish with remaining spice.

5. Reduce grill heat to medium-low. Drizzle fish with oil on both sides and place on grill or on a broiler pan covered with aluminum foil.

6. Let grill or broil for about 7–10 minutes for each side, checking occasionally until light brown and cooked. Then flip the fish to grill the opposite side.

7. The grilled Tilapia is ready to bring joy to the table. Enjoy this freshly grilled fish with some hot Kenkey.

Shrimp Something

Serves: 4

Prep Time: 10 minutes

Cooking Time: 15 minutes

Oh, isn't that something!

For any young African professional with a New York state of mind. Something simple, light, and quick for anyone who wants to eat and dream of a fresh, wholesome dish with an inviting Tropical Ghana aroma that fills the mind with joyful melodies. Can onions not play with shrimp inside the food playground? This fresh, sizzling shrimp recipe pairs well with grilled plantains and avocado; though on its own, it can help you settle back into your groove after a long day or from jetlag. Wow! That's something!

For Shrimp
- 1lb (16oz/454g) shrimp, cleaned, peeled, deveined
- ½ tsp black pepper
- 1 tsp salt

For Something Mix
- 1 large yellow onion (10oz/284g), chopped
- 4 cloves garlic, finely chopped
- 4oz (113g) ginger root, peeled, minced
- 1 tsp crushed red pepper
- 2½ tsp dry dill weed
- 10 fresh basil leaves
- 3½ tbsp olive oil

Preparation

1. In a sauté pan, combine olive oil and yellow onion over high heat for about 3 minutes, stirring continuously.

2. Add garlic and continue stirring for another 5–7 minutes.

3. As yellow onion and garlic sizzles, season shrimp with black pepper and salt.

4. Add seasoned shrimp to onion mix when onion bits soften and begin to turn golden brown on the edges.

5. Reduce heat to medium. Add ginger and stir for about 2 minutes. Then add crushed red pepper and dill weed. Continue stirring for about 4 minutes or until shrimp is cooked.

6. Turn heat off and plate your shrimp. Chiffonade the basil leaves and garnish shrimp. Time to eat!

> **Tip: Kick it up a notch!**
> Double or triple the amount of crushed red pepper to give it a serious kick.

Grilled Fish, Ghana Fisherman Style

Serves: 6 | Prep Time: 10 minutes | Cooking Time: 15 minutes

One of the best-kept Tropical Ghana secrets is out! Fishermen in Ghana, who are fortunate to have been let in on this secret by their fathers, grandfathers, and great grandfathers know to include Asanka (clay grinding bowl), salt, pepper, ginger and a portable stove, in addition to their fishing gear when they set out to sea in their canoes. When combined skillfully, these items and a fresh catch of fish yields a mouth-watering grilled fish dish that sends you to a new fishing level. Your turn to join them on land, in your own home or off your boat somewhere else. It's time to let this mouth-watering recipe take you on a whole new journey!

For Fish
• 1 large (2lbs/1kg) whole Bronzini/Bronzino or Tilapia or Red Snapper, scaled, gutted and cleaned
• 1 tsp salt

For Ghana Fisherman Spice
• 2 tbsp olive oil (or vegetable oil)
• 2½ tbsp (4oz/113g) ginger root, peeled and freshly minced
• 2 tbsp crushed red pepper (chilli pepper flakes)

> **Tip: Extra mild or extra hot**
> For extra mild, add a tablespoon ginger or a tablespoon more of crushed red pepper to increase the pepper heat level.

Preparation
1. Preheat grill or turn on the broiler of your cooking unit.

2. On a chopping board, score fish on both sides or gently cut four diagonal slashes on each side of the fish or shallow cuts, just shy of reaching the bone.

3. Salt the fish. Combine ginger and crushed red pepper in a small bowl and mix completely.

4. Using your fingers, fill the slashes or cavities on skin first with the spice. Then coat inside and the rest of the fish with remaining spice.

5. Reduce grill heat to medium-low. Drizzle fish with oil on both sides and place on grill or on a broiler pan with grate.

6. Let grill or broil for about 7–10 minutes for each side, checking occasionally until light brown and cooked. Then flip the fish to grill the opposite side.

7. Serve this tasty, mouth-watering fish with avocado slices and sides of choice.

Shitɔ Lo/Charcoal Grilled Mackerel

Serves: 6 | Prep Time: 10 minutes | Cooking Time: 15 minutes

Shitɔ Lo is a charcoal grill item that must be on all serious night fish grill stands unless the demand on a particular night outweighs supply. Shitɔ means pepper in the Ga language and Lo is fish, so Shitɔ Lo is pepper's fish or pepper's companion fish in English. The English translation does not convey the love, passion, and excitement associated with Shitɔ Lo. It's best enjoyed with its companions of freshly ground pepper from the Asanka and obviously hot Kenkey. The Ga ladies who grill close to the coast at night in Accra know how to put happy smiles on faces with hot Shitɔ Lo.

For Fish
• 3 medium whole Mackerel, scaled, gutted, cleaned
• 1¾ tsp salt

For Grilling
• 2 tbsp vegetable oil

For Shitɔ Lo Marinade
• 1 small (4oz/113g) yellow onion, peeled
• 6oz (170g) ginger root, peeled
• 4 cloves garlic
• 25 Kpakpo Shitɔ (20 Scotch Bonnet/15 Habanero) pepper

Tip: Marinade overnight
Let the spice stay on overnight for a more intense Shitɔ Lo.

Preparation

1. Preheat grill or turn on the broiler of your cooking unit.

2. On a chopping board, score fish on both sides or gently cut two or three slashes across the length on each side of the fish or shallow cuts, just shy of reaching the bone. Then salt the fish.

3. Combine the Shitɔ Lo spice ingredients in a blender or food processor into paste.

Alternatively, the earthenware grinding bowl with its wooden masher can be used to combine the spice ingredients into a paste.

4. Using your fingers, fill the slashes or cavities on skin first with the spice. Generously coat inside and the rest of the fish with remaining spice.

5. Reduce grill heat to medium-low. Drizzle fish with oil on both sides and place on grill or on a broiler pan with grate.

6. Let grill or broil for about 7–10 minutes for each side, checking until light brown and cooked. Then flip the fish to grill the other side.

7. Ready or not, Shitɔ Lo is ready for some lovely, delicious action. It is best enjoyed with hot Kenkey and freshly ground Kpakpo Shitɔ (Shito).

Aklɔ/Aklor

Serves: 6 | Prep Time: 10 minutes | Cooking Time: 15 minutes

Aklɔ/Aklor (pronounced "ah-claw") is a quick a fresh steamed fish infused with peppers, onions, herbs, and spices of choice. Aklɔ translates loosely from the Ga language to "let's pick up" – something along the lines of "let's pick up the steamed hot fish to enjoy." It's a coastal recipe off of the canoes of Ga-Adangbe fishermen who either steam the fish in their canoes at sea or right on arrival. Fresh herrings are well known for this recipe, but many other kinds of fish can be used. Others prefer a larger fish to deal with the least amount of fish bones compared to herrings.

For Sweet Steam

• 1lb (16oz/454g) fresh herrings (sardines, whiting or fish of choice) scaled, gutted, cleaned, cut into two

• 1 large red onion (12oz/340g), thinly sliced rings

• 12 Kpakpo Shitɔ (Pettie Belle Pepper), sliced (or 7 Scotch Bonnet /4 Habanero) pepper

• 4 cloves garlic, finely chopped

• 4 tsp ginger, freshly minced

• 1½ tsp salt

• 2 dry bay leaves, crushed

• 4 tbsp water

Preparation

1. Place herrings in a saucepan. Top with red onion, ginger, garlic, Kpakpo Shitɔ (Scotch Bonnet) and salt. Cover saucepan with lid and let steam for about 9–12 minutes over medium heat.

2. Remove from fire and serve Akloo with side of choice or enjoy as is – steaming and hot.

Tip 1: Try with shallots
Replace the red onions with shallots and give the recipe a little more of a youthful kick or milder onion kick.

Tip 2: Mild or spicy option
Reduce or add more Kpakpo Shitɔ or Scotch Bonnet pepper to increase the pepper heat level to your taste.

Aklɔ Brodo/Ghana Sea Sandwich

Serves: 6 | Prep Time: 10 minutes | Sandwich Time: 5 minutes

When Aklɔ is ready, it can be taken one more step. Once the bones are removed and the fish goes into bread, it becomes Aklɔ Brodo, which is an Aklɔ sandwich. Brodo means bread in the Ga language. Use the onions, peppers, garlic bits, herbs, and juice from the steam pan as topping for the sandwich. Aklɔ Brodo is the original Ghana Sea Sandwich, and any true fishing family passes their own version with unique spices from one generation to another. Bite into and enjoy this fresh, sweet steam in sandwich form.

For Sandwich Bread

• 12 slices of fresh bread of choice (or 2 round fresh bread rolls or 2 long fresh hero rolls, halved)

For Optional Extra Veg Topping

• 2 carrots, cleaned and curled with a peeler into 2½-inch length ribbons

• 1 avocado, peeled, sliced

• 3 spring onions (scallions), cleaned, with white part freshly chopped

Preparation

1. Debone Aklɔ (steamed fish) and discard bones.

2. Grab bread of choice, slice open, and lightly toast if preferred.

3. Scoop Aklɔ and evenly distribute on 6 bread rolls. Add the steamed onions, peppers, garlic bits, herbs, and juice from the steam pan on top.

4. You are set to enjoy Aklɔ Brodo (the original Ghana Sea Sandwich) with drink or top with optional extra veg topping to take it to another level.

5. It's right in your hands to finalize this plot and enjoy this fresh sea sandwich.

KIH-KENKEY IS HOT! WHERE'S THE PEPPER?

K-I-H! Kenkey is hot! K-I-H! Kenkey is hot! K-I-H! Kenkey is hot! Where is the pepper?

It sounds like a political campaign slogan, but it's from the Tropical Ghana kitchen and for any day when the task at hand needs a morale booster for the team. It stems from how folks react in the Ga language – "Komi Kala Kala" (hot, steaming Kenkey).

We love Kenkey. It best served steaming hot. Kenkey, also known as Komi or Otimi (Ga-Adangbe) or Dokono (Akan), is a commodity that is needed whenever fish is present. Aside fish, it goes well with several stews too. But fish and Kenkey go hand in hand. The two popular ones are the Ga Kenkey in corn husk and Fante Kenkey in plantain or banana leaves.

Made out of corn or maize, Kenkey goes through a few processes including soaking, grinding, and fermenting. This ball of goodness is made by experts and we leave it to them to continue the tradition that runs in the family. The secret recipe is passed on from one generation to another. Oftentimes, new players attempt their version, but a true Kenkey expert will smoke them out and immediately know that it is from a rookie player. When you find your Kenkey-selling family, you stay loyal to keep your taste buds and tummy happy.

Ga Kenkey.

Fante Kenkey.

Banku.

You cannot talk about Kenkey and forget Banku. Banku is like the eldest sibling of Kenkey. Although it is also made from ground corn that has been soaked with water to create corn dough, it undergoes less processes. Additionally, ground Cassava (Yuca) turned into dough can also be used. Some people prefer a mix of corn and Cassava dough Banku. Banku is the preferred go-to favourite for eating Okro Soup and Okro Stew.

Aboloo.

Aboloo is the other member of the corn dough family for enjoying fried fish and stews. There are at least three kinds of Aboloo: the Steamed Ewe Aboloo, Baked Ga Aboloo, and the Baked Fante Aboloo.

Steamed Ewe Aboloo

Baked Ga Aboloo

Shitɔ.
Ground
Pepper.

And then, there's Shitɔ!

In Ghana, Kenkey and Banku lovers know that the second thing after getting hot Kenkey or Banku is its best companion Shitɔ (freshly ground pepper). It is a must-have, even if there's no fish available because grinding fresh Shitɔ will take you far to enjoy many meals and beyond.

GHANAIAN STAPLES, TUBERS, ROOT VEGETABLES & PALS

Roots and tubers in Ghana are usually cooked together, by mixing and matching, or even cooked with plantains. You can boil Ghana Yam, Plantain, Kooko (Taro), Cocoyam, Sweet Potato (Batata), and Cassava (Yuca) together, or Plantain and Cassava or Ghana Yam and Plantain, or simply any of them alone.

Ghana Yams come in variety with sweetness. These tasty root vegetables are staples that go well with stews and soups, featuring everyday on plates across the country. Fried Ghana Yam and Sweet Potatoes are popular street food enjoyed all over with fried Kooko (Taro) and Cocoyam also in that department when available.

Yellow Sweet Potatoes

Red Sweet Potatoes

Tuber of Ghana Yam

Boiled Cocoyam & Ghana Yam

Boiled Taro

Cut Ghana Yam

Boiled Sweet Potatoes

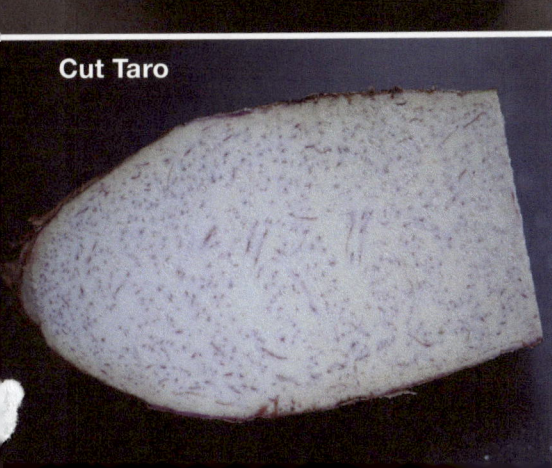

Cut Taro

Cassava

Fufu.

Fufu is Ghana's wonder complement side to every soup except for Okro Soup. It is made in a pestle and mortar with either boiled green Plantain or Ghana Yam or Cocoyam (Yautia) or Cassava (Yuca) or a mix of any of them as preferred. Modern versions are available in powdered form, but many agree the original is the original. Fufu is enjoyed with any soup any day.

Kokonte. Face The Wall.

Kokonte is the powdered form of ground sun-dried Cassava (Yuca), and nicknamed "Face The Wall" when cooked. Some say the name is derived from the fact that there's no uniformity in getting a rather perfect shape when serving. Hence folks hide by facing the wall direction in Chop Bars so their dining is out of sight. However, this is a disputed theory as the lovers of Face The Wall say. It's because it offers a precious and delicious experience, they don't want to share.

Face The Wall is delicious and comes in a rustic golden hue which is achieved when good-quality Cassava (Yuca) is used and the sun-drying process is done correctly. It's a delicacy that goes very well with Groundnut Soup. Okro Soup is another option. It's easy to find powder packs of Kokonte with instructions on how to make Face The Wall.

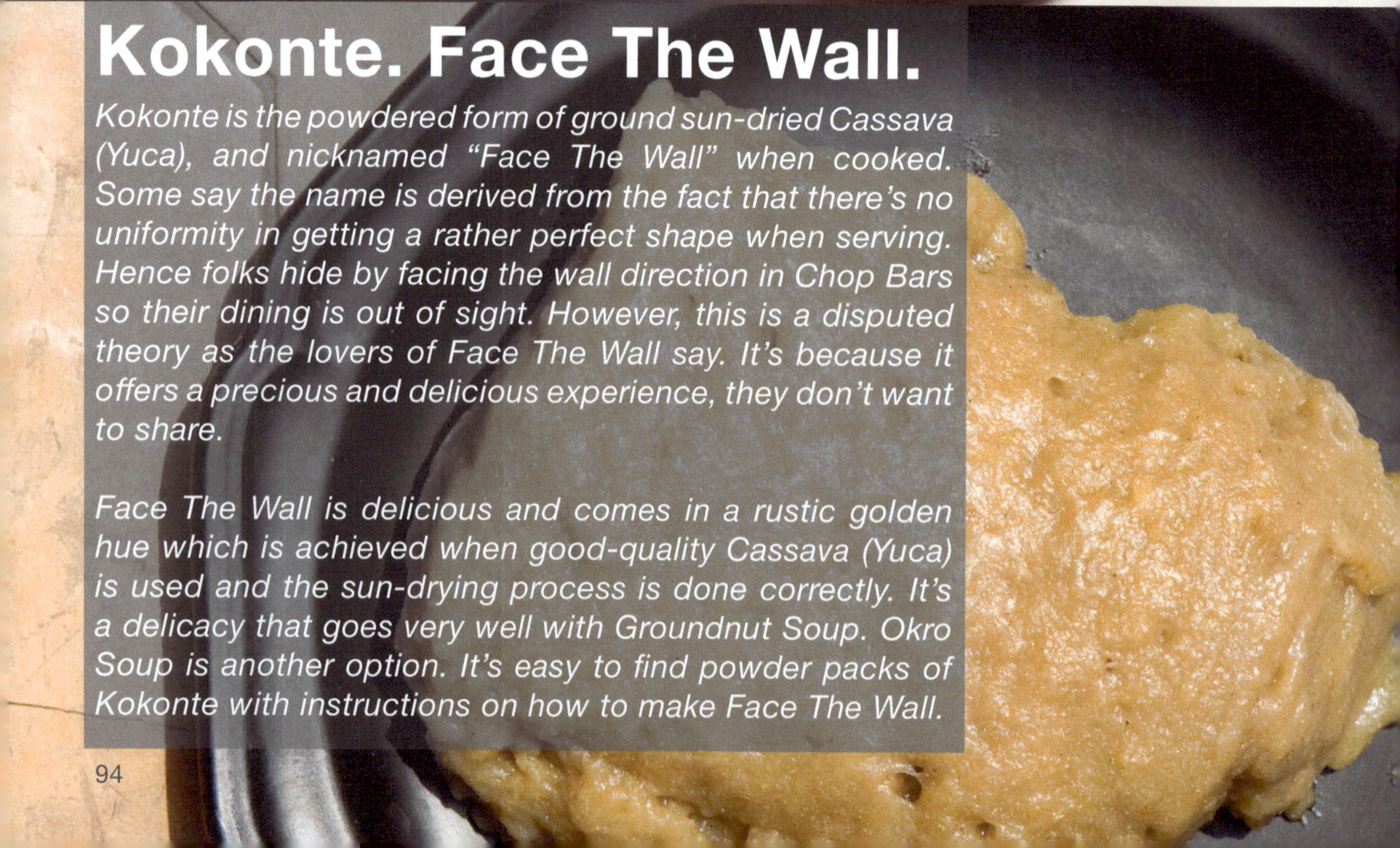

Yam Otɔ/ Yam Etɔ

Serves: 6

Prep Time: 10 minutes

Cooking Time: 25 minutes

Say "oh-tor" or "er-tor." Yam Otɔ or Yam Etɔ is a very simple and easy-to-make meal for everyday, and also for occasions and events. All the action happens in the Asanka.

For Cooking Yam
- ½ medium tuber (3lbs/1.3kg) Ghana Yam (West African Yam)
- 4½ cups (36oz/1L) water
- 1½ tsp salt

For Boiling Eggs
- 6 eggs
- 3 cups (25fl oz/750ml) water
- 1 tsp salt

For Zomi Stew
- 6 tbsp (3fl oz/89ml) Zomi (spiced palm oil)
- 1 small (4oz/113g) tomato, blended
- 1 small yellow onion (4oz/113g), finely chopped
- ½ Scotch Bonnet (Habanero) pepper, finely chopped
- 1 clove garlic, finely chopped
- ½ tsp minced ginger
- 1 tsp dried shrimp powder
- ½ tsp salt

Preparation

1. Peel and cut yam to about 2x4-inches sizes. Place in a large cooking pot, add water, and bring to boil over medium-high heat for about 20–25 minutes.

2. Place eggs into another cooking pot, add water, and let boil over medium heat for 15 minutes. Remove eggs into a bowl of tap water to cool.

3. Meanwhile, warm palm oil in a saucepan over medium heat. Add Scotch Bonnet, red onion, ginger, garlic, and salt. Stir continuously for about 5–8 minutes.

4. Add tomatoes and mix completely. Cover saucepan with lid and let cook for about 5 minutes.

5. Add dried shrimp powder and stir continuously for 2 minutes.

6. Reduce heat to the lowest and simmer for 5 minutes uncovered. Turn heat off.

7. Check yam for tenderness with a fork. If fork slides easily into the yam, it's cooked, exactly how one cooks potatoes. Drain water and mash yam hot. Yam is mashed traditionally in the clay grinding bowl, Asanka, with a wooden grinder. If available, use an Asanka.

8. Add Zomi Stew into mashed yam and mix through and through. Peel eggs and cut in half or quarters. Garnish Yam Otor with eggs and serve.

> **Tip: Use Cocoyam instead of Ghana Yam**
> Cut Cocoyam into quarters and follow the same steps as for Ghana Yam.

GREEN KONTOMIRE & THE VEGETABLE PLOT

Ghanaians love their greens and the most famous is Kontomire (pronounced "con-tor-mi-ray"). Fresh Kontomire brings so much joy and adds to the diet of most Ghanaians in their stew preparations and more. As the number one well-known green in Ghana, it does wonders in different forms. Besides Kontomire, others such as Spinach, Borkorborkor (Waterleaf), leaves from the Garden Eggs plant, Okro plant, Cassava leaf, Ademe (Jute leaves) Baobab leaves and more all feature. Other vegetables such as Okro (Okra), Garden Eggs (Eggplant), Abedru (Turkey Berry/Wild Eggplant) and others are close to Kontomire, like cousins from the same farm, and play a significant role in the cooking pots and saucepans across Ghana.

Abedru (Turkey Berry/Wild Eggplant)

Okro & Garden Eggs

Abom/Kontomire Stew/ Palava Sauce/Spinach Stew: A Powerhouse Stew Family

Kontomire is the Ghanaian name for the leaves of the Cocoyam plant, a member of the Taro plant family. The stew is a simple and wholesome go-to recipe among farming communities that cultivate root crops in Ghana. The main ingredient of the stew is Kontomire, and it pairs well with boiled Cocoyam or the root of the same plant. It is widely eaten with boiled Ghana Yam and green plantains. Traditionally, the leaves are steamed. As the leaves steam, fresh ground pepper is made from a combination of Odjɛŋma (Scotch Bonnet), onions, tomatoes and salt in an Asanka (clay grinding bowl). The steamed Kontomire is added right off the fire into the pepper mixture and ground to a desired texture. It's immediately drizzled with palm oil. The palm oil melts into the warm Kontomire mix and presents a fresh, tasty bowl of steamed Kontomire as everyone partakes in this delicious communal meal.

Overtime, the traditional Kontomire born in the Asanka (clay grinding bowl), known as Abom, evolved and a stew version overtook the original traditional version. Moreover, a second form of the stew called Palava Sauce emerged. When the seeds of a squash variety found in West Africa called Agushi (Egusi or Melon Seeds) are added to the Kontomire stew during cooking, it becomes Palava Sauce. Today, whether enjoying Kontomire Stew or Palava Sauce, it can be made with any mix of meats including beef, tripe, smoked fish or shrimp, salted Tilapia as well as boiled eggs or without the meats. The stew is popularly enjoyed with boiled Cocoyam, Taro, Ghana Yam (West African Yam), Sweet Potato, Plantain and Cassava. Since Kontomire or Taro leaves are not easily found in all parts of the world, Spinach leaves are usually used as a substitute. It's time to experience the power of this stew powerhouse!

Steamed Kontomire

Mashed Kontomire

Abom

Serves: 6
Prep Time: 10 minutes
Cooking Time: 15 minutes

For Abom

• 3 bunches/2¼lbs (36oz/1Kg) Kontomire or Taro leaves, trimmed
• 9 tbsp (4½fl oz/133ml palm oil
• 1 medium red onion (8oz/227g), sliced
• 3 Scotch Bonnet (Habanero) pepper
• 1 large tomatoes (½lb/227g)
• ½lb (8oz/227g) smoked mackerel, tuna, herrings, or a mix of all
• 1 large Koobi (salt-preserved dried Tilapia), gills removed, lightly rinsed to remove excess salt, pat dry, cut into 4–6 pieces

> **Tip 1: Raise the temperature or!**
> Add extra Scotch Bonnet (Habanero) pepper to increase the pepper heat level or reduce to bring the heat level low.

> **Tip 2: Make it vegetarian**
> Omit the Koobi and any meat.

Preparation

1. Roast the whole tomato over open flame or a grill, turning all sides till skin is lightly charred all around. Set tomato aside on a plate.

2. Grab a Ghana earthenware grinding bowl (Asanka), put Scotch Bonnet and onions, and use the wooden masher to crush and mash it together. Remove charred tomato skin, add tomato, and keep crushing and mixing all into paste.

3. Dip the Kontomire in a bowl of water with salt and wash. Remove and shake water off. Place in a saucepan to steam over medium heat for about 5 minutes. Shaking off water helps to steam the Kontomire in the least amount of water so in the end no juice is left and the Abom is not watery.

4. Meanwhile, place Koobi pieces on a grill over medium heat for about 10–12 minutes, 5–6 minutes on each side or until golden brown and done.

5. Pour steamed Kontomire into clay grinding bowl over the Scotch Bonnet, onion, and tomato mix. Continue to mash and mix thoroughly.

6. Pour palm oil over Kontomire mash and mix, as the steam from the mash helps warm the palm oil and melt it into the Abom.

7. Add the grilled Koobi pieces and smoked mackerel, tuna, or herrings. Enjoy the Abom with freshly boiled Ghana Yam (West African Yam), Cocoyam, plantains, or a combination of all.

Kontomire Stew

Serves: 6 | **Prep Time:** 10 minutes | **Cooking Time:** 40 minutes

For Frying Koobi

• 2 medium Koobi (salt-preserved dried Tilapia), gills removed, lightly rinsed to remove excess salt, pat dry, cut into 6 pieces
• 9 tbsp (4½fl oz/133ml) palm oil

For Stew Base

• 1 medium red onion (8oz/227g), sliced
• 1-inch cube size cut of Loo Shala (Momoni/Stinky Fish), rinse, pat dry
• 2 Scotch Bonnet (Habanero) pepper, finely chopped
• 2 large tomatoes (1lb/454g), chopped
• 4 cloves garlic, sliced lengthwise
• 5 tsp ginger, freshly minced
• 1 tsp tomato puree (or paste)
• 2 tsp smoked shrimp or fish powder
• ½lb (8oz/227g) smoked mackerel, tuna, herrings, or mix of all

For Kontomire

• 3 bunches/2¼lbs (36oz/1Kg) Kontomire or Taro leaves, washed in salt in water, trimmed, freshly chopped

Preparation

1. Warm palm oil in a saucepan over medium heat and fry Koobi for about 8–10 minutes, 4–5 minutes on each side. Save on a plate. Add red onion, ginger, garlic, Scotch Bonnet and Loo Shala (Momoni/ Stinky Fish) to palm oil for about 8 minutes, stirring continuously.

2. Add tomato puree to sizzling mix when onion softens and begins to turn golden brown on the edges. Continue stirring for about 2 minutes, mixing in puree.

3. Add chopped tomatoes and mix completely. Cover saucepan with lid, turn heat to high, and let cook.

4. After 5 minutes reduce heat to medium and tip lid slightly so saucepan is partly covered to allow some steam to escape. Let simmer for 5 minutes, stirring occasionally. Then add smoked shrimp and fish powder and mix completely.

5. Reduce heat to low and let simmer 5 more minutes. Add smoked fish and Koobi and continue to stir for 2 minutes. Add chopped Kontomire or Taro leaves. Mix completely and replace saucepan lid and let cook for 5 minutes.

6. Remove from fire and uncover. Grab your plates and enjoy this stew paired with your favourite side.

Palava Sauce

Serves: 6 | **Prep Time:** 10 minutes | **Cooking Time:** 50 minutes

For Kontomire
• 3 bunches/2¼lbs (36oz/1Kg) Kontomire or Taro leaves, washed in salt in water, trimmed, freshly chopped

For Frying Koobi
• 2 medium Koobi (salt-preserved dried Tilapia), gills removed, lightly rinsed to remove excess salt, pat dry, cut into 6 pieces
• 9 tbsp (4½fl oz/133ml) palm oil

For Palava Action
• 12 tbsp (6oz/120g) Agushi/Egusi (melon seeds or raw shelled pumpkin seeds)
• 5 tbsp water

For Stew Base
• 1 medium red onion (8oz/227g), sliced
• 2 Scotch Bonnet (Habanero) pepper, finely chopped
• 2 large tomatoes (1lb/454g), chopped
• 4 cloves garlic, finely chopped
• 5 tsp ginger, freshly minced
• 1 tsp tomato puree (or paste)
• 2 tsp smoked shrimp or fish powder
• ½lb (8oz/227g) smoked mackerel, tuna, herrings, or a mix of all

Preparation

1. In a saucepan, warm palm oil over medium heat and fry Koobi for about 8–10 minutes, 4–5 minutes on each side. Save on a plate. Add red onion, ginger, garlic, Scotch Bonnet and Loo Shala (Momoni/Stinky Fish) to palm oil for about 8 minutes, stirring continuously.

2. Add tomato puree to sizzling mix when onion softens and begins to turn golden brown on the edges. Continue stirring for about 2 minutes, mixing in puree. Add chopped tomatoes and mix completely. Cover saucepan with lid, turn heat to high, and let cook.

3. Meanwhile, pulse Agushi or pumpkin seeds in small amounts in a blender or food processor into a texture similar to raw sugar.

4. After 5 minutes reduce heat to medium and tip lid slightly so saucepan is partly covered to allow some steam to escape. Let simmer for 5 minutes, stirring occasionally.

5. Add smoked shrimp or fish powder and mix completely. Reduce heat to low and continue to stir for about 2 minutes. Add smoked fish and Koobi and continue to stir for 2 minutes.

6. In a small bowl, add water in tablespoon increments to blended Agushi or pumpkin seeds and stir until it comes together to form a smooth paste. Add paste to stew, cover with lid and continue to cook for about 10 minutes.

7. Stir stew and add chopped Kontomire or Taro leaves, sprinkle with a tablespoon of water and mix completely. Replace saucepan lid and let cook for 5 minutes.

8. Remove from fire and uncover. It's time to enjoy some Palava Sauce with your favourite sides.

> **Tip: Rejuvenate and warm Agushi (melon seeds)!**
> In a large frying pan, dry-toast the Agushi (melon seeds) for about 2–3 minutes or until golden brown and fragrant. Remove from fire and set aside to cool before pulsing in blender to use in stew.

Spinach Stew

Serves: 6 | **Prep Time:** 10 minutes | **Cooking Time:** 35 minutes

For Spinach

• 2 bunches (24oz/680g) spinach, washed, trimmed, and freshly chopped

For Stew Base

• 8 medium tomatoes (2lbs/1kg), chopped
• 1 large red onion (12oz/340g), thinly sliced
• 1 Scotch Bonnet (Habanero) pepper, finely chopped
• 4 cloves garlic, finely chopped
• 2 tsp ginger, freshly minced
• 10 tbsp (5fl oz/148ml) vegetable oil or 9 tbsp (4½fl oz/133ml) palm oil
• 2 tsp salt
• 2 tsp tomato puree (or paste)

Preparation

1. In a saucepan combine oil, red onion, ginger, garlic, Scotch Bonnet and salt over high heat for about 5–7 minutes, stirring continuously.

2. Add tomato puree to sizzling mix when onion bits soften and begin to turn golden brown on the edges. Continue stirring for about 2 minutes, mixing in puree.

3. Add chopped tomatoes and mix completely. Cover saucepan with lid, turn the heat to high, and let cook.

4. After 5 minutes reduce heat to medium and tip lid slightly to partly cover saucepan to allow some steam to escape. Let stew cook for 10 minutes, stirring occasionally.

5. Reduce heat to low and let simmer for about 5 minutes. Then add spinach and mix completely. Replace saucepan lid and let cook for 5 minutes.

6. Remove from fire and turn fire off. Grab your plates and enjoy this stew paired with your favorite side.

Kontomire Family Stew Tips

Tip 1: Boiled whole eggs can add a touch!
Though smoked fish such mackerel and white tuna together with Koobi are most popular in Kontomire and Palava Sauce, boiled whole eggs also feature prominently and add a touch to the stew. Boiled whole eggs are added at the end when the stew is off the fire or right before serving the stew.

Tip 2: Other meats can be added too!
Beef, beef tripe, and Wele (preserved cow hide) are favourites that are added to Kontomire and Palava Sauce too. Feel free to add meats of your choice. Steam meats before adding to the stew. Meats should be added 5 minutes before adding the smoked fish or shrimp powder.

Garden Eggs Stew

Serves: 6
Prep Time: 10 minutes
Cooking Time: 45 minutes

In honour of the late Beatrice Naa Koshie Glover, a stew expert.

For Garden Eggs

- 1½lbs (24oz/680g) white Garden Eggs (white eggplants) washed, stems trimmed, each cut into quarters
- 8 tbsp (½cup/4fl oz) water

For Fish

- 2 tsp smoked shrimp or fish powder
- ½lb (8oz/227g) smoked mackerel, trout, tuna, herrings, or a mix of all
- 1 large Koobi (Salt Preserved Dried Tilapia), gills removed, lightly rinsed to remove excess salt, pat dry, cut into 6 pieces

For Stew

- 9 tbsp (4½fl oz/133ml) palm oil
- 1-inch cube size Loo Shala (Momoni/Stinky Fish), rinse, pat dry
- 1 medium yellow onion (8oz/227g), sliced
- 2 Scotch Bonnet (Habanero) pepper, finely chopped
- 2 large tomatoes (1lb/454g), chopped
- 4 cloves garlic, finely chopped
- 5 tsp ginger, freshly minced
- 1 tsp tomato puree (or paste)

> **Tip 1: No salt please! Koobi is salt preserved dried tilapia!**
> The way Koobi is preserved with salt makes the dried fish retain most of the salt even after a light rinse with water. When used in a stew, no salt should be added because Koobi contains enough salt.

Preparation

1. Steam white Garden Eggs with 8 tablespoons water in a cooking pot with a tight-fitting lid over medium heat for about 5–7 minutes or until tender. Partially uncover and set aside to cool.

2. Meanwhile, warm palm oil in a saucepan over medium heat and fry Koobi for about 8–10 minutes, 4–5 minutes on each side. Save on a plate. Add onion, ginger, garlic, Scotch Bonnet and Loo Shala to palm oil for about 5–6 minutes, stirring continuously.

3. Add tomato puree to sizzling mix when onion softens and begin to turn golden brown on the edges. Continue stirring for about 2 minutes, mixing in puree.

4. Add chopped tomatoes and mix completely. Cover saucepan with lid, turn heat to high and let cook.

5. As stew cooks, grab a Ghana earthenware grinding bowl (Asanka). Remove the thin skin off steamed white Garden Eggs. Place in the Asanka and use the wooden masher to crush and mash it together.

> **Tip 2: Raise the temperature or!**
> Add extra Scotch Bonnet (Habanero) pepper to increase the heat level or reduce the Scotch Bonnet to bring the heat level down.

Alternatively, a food processor can be used to mash the white Garden Eggs by pulsing on and off for about a minute or two.

6. After 5 minutes reduce stew heat to medium and tip lid slightly so saucepan is partly covered to allow some steam to escape. Let simmer for 2 minutes, stirring occasionally. Then add smoked shrimp or fish powder and mix completely.

7. Reduce heat to low and let continue to simmer 3 more minutes. Add smoked fish and fried Koobi, continue to stir for 2 minutes.

8. Add mashed white Garden Eggs. Mix completely and replace saucepan lid and let simmer for 5 minutes on lowest heat.

9. Uncover, stir one last time and turn the heat off. It's time to enjoy this stew by pairing it with your favorite side or sides. Nevertheless, it's best enjoyed with a varieties of freshly boiled tender root vegetables such West African yam, cocoyam, taro, plantain, sweet potatoes and Cassava.

> **Tip 3: Other dried salted fish like Baccala can be substituted for Koobi**
> Other dried salted like Baccala can be used when you cannot find Koobi.

Okro Stew

Serves: 6 | **Prep Time:** 10 minutes | **Cooking Time:** 65 minutes

Okro is that vegetable when cut lets out its slippery juice. When you are called "Okro-mouth" in Ghana, it means everything just slips out of your mouth. Yep, you cannot keep things to yourself especially any juicy gossip. A good plate of Okro Stew shared with friends can make you spill the beans without any prompting. Even the "toughest of toughest" can sometimes be broken and some secrets extracted from them with Okro Stew. Watch out before you get caught up spilling the beans.

Okro Stew hits all the spots, with its deep flavour, richness in texture, and pool of meat varieties. Okro Stew's best companion is hot Banku. It goes well with other sides, too. Some folks believe the next morning after the stew is made is a day of renewed joy as the stew taste even better because all of the ingredients are well-integrated. One thing is for sure – Okro Stew comes multi-layered with a taste that can get you in a good mood.

For Okro Mix
- 1½lb (24oz/680g) Okro (Okra), washed, chopped fresh
- 1lb (16oz/454g) white Garden Eggs or white eggplant, washed, chopped fresh
- 8tbsp (½ cup/4oz) water

For Tomato Base

- 9 tbsp (4½fl oz/133ml) palm oil
- 2 large tomatoes (1lb/454g), finely chopped
- 1 medium (6oz/170g) yellow onion, thinly sliced
- 2 Scotch Bonnet (Habanero) pepper, sliced
- 5 cloves garlic, finely chopped
- 5 tsp ginger root, finely chopped
- 2 tsp salt
- 1 tsp tomato puree (or paste)
- 2 tsp smoked shrimp or fish powder

For Meats/Fish

- 1lb (16oz/454g) fresh lamb or mutton or beef, clean, trimmed of excess fat, chopped to bite-sizes
- ½lb (8oz/227g) fresh African giant snails, de-shelled, cleaned with lemon juice
- ½lb (8oz/227g) Wele (preserved cow hide), cleaned
- 6 live land or blue crabs or sea crabs, rinsed, steamed, legs' pointy tips broken off
- ½lb (8oz/227g) smoked mackerel, tuna, herrings, or a mix of all
- 4 cloves garlic, finely chopped
- 1 small (4oz/113g) red onion, finely chopped
- 2 tsp salt
- 1 tsp white or black pepper
- 2 tsp minced ginger
- 1 ½ cups water

Preparation

1. Parboil Okro mix ingredients in a cooking pot over high heat for about 5–7 minutes. Uncover and set aside to cool.

2. Combine mutton red onion, garlic, ginger, and white pepper in a pot over high heat. Add a teaspoon of salt and stir frequently, for about 5 minutes, to keep meat from sticking to bottom of cooking pot, until onions soften and mutton starts browning and letting out its natural juice. Cover pot and let steam for 3 minutes. Turn heat off, set aside, and uncover till it cools. Then recover with lid.

3. Place fresh snails and ½ cup of water in a small pan over high heat for 5 minutes to steam snails. Save any remaining liquid.

4. In a large saucepan warm palm oil over medium heat. Add red onion, ginger, garlic, Scotch Bonnet and rest of salt into palm oil. Stir continuously for about 7–10 minutes.

5. Add tomato puree when onion bits soften and begin to turn golden brown on the edges. Continue stirring for about a minute, mixing in puree.

6. Add chopped tomatoes and mix completely. Cover saucepan with lid, turn heat to medium-high, and let cook. After 10 minutes, add the mutton with its stock into the tomato stew. Partly cover saucepan and let stew continue to cook for 10 minutes, stirring occasionally.

7. Boil Wele with 1 cup water over high heat for about 10 minutes. Drain liquid after and discard.

8. Introduce the Wele and steamed crabs into the stew for about 2 minutes. Then add the snails with any remaining snail liquid residue and mix thoroughly into stew. Reduce heat to medium and let simmer 5 minutes. Add fish or shrimp powder and stir completely.

9. After 2 minutes, add the parboiled Okro and Garden Eggs and mix thoroughly. Break smoked mackerel and herring into bite-size pieces and mix into stew. Partly cover the saucepan, reduce heat to low and let simmer for 10 minutes.

10. Turn fire off. It's time to enjoy some Ghana Okro Stew with some Banku or any other cooked roots and tubers of choice.

Tip: Raise the temperature or not!
Add extra Scotch Bonnet (Habanero) pepper to increase the pepper heat level or reduce the Scotch Bonnet to bring the heat level down.

Okro Stew – No Palm Oil

Serves: 6 | **Prep Time:** 10 minutes | **Cooking Time:** 65 minutes

Some say the no-palm-oil Okro Stew is for the days when you run out of palm oil, even though that barely happens in Ghanaian homes.

The second version of Okro Stew uses vegetable oil instead of palm oil and is preferred by some Ghanaians. Though not the most popular option, this no-palm-oil version does a wonderful job with the essential building blocks of a Ghanaian Okro Stew.

Try it out and you'll realize the value is the same, the smile will most likely be the same, and the crowd will still gather.

For Okro Mix

- 1½lb (24oz/680g) Okro (Okra), washed, chopped fresh
- 1lb (16oz/454g) white Garden Eggs or white eggplant, washed, chopped fresh
- 8 tbsp (½ cup/4oz) water

For Tomato Base

- 10 tbsp (5fl oz/148ml) vegetable oil
- 2 large tomatoes (1lb/454g), finely chopped
- 1 medium (6oz/170g) yellow onion, thinly sliced
- 2 Scotch Bonnet (Habanero) pepper, sliced
- 5 cloves garlic, finely chopped
- 5 tsp ginger root, finely chopped
- 2 tsp salt
- 1 tsp tomato puree (or paste)
- 2 tsp smoked shrimp or fish powder

For Meats/Fish

- 1lb (16oz/454g) fresh lamb or mutton or beef, clean, trimmed of excess fat, chopped to bite-sizes
- ½lb (8oz/227g) fresh African giant snails, de-shelled, cleaned with lemon juice
- ½lb (8oz/227g) Wele (preserved cow hide), cleaned
- 6 live land or blue crabs or sea crabs, rinsed, steamed, legs' pointy tips broken off
- ½lb (8oz/227g) smoked mackerel, tuna, herrings, or a mix of all
- 4 cloves garlic, finely chopped
- 1 small (4oz/113g) red onion, finely chopped
- 2 tsp salt
- 1 tsp white or black pepper
- 2 tsp minced ginger
- 1½ cups water

Preparation

1. Parboil Okro mix ingredients in a cooking pot over high heat for about 5–7 minutes. Uncover and set aside to cool.

2. Meanwhile, combine mutton, red onion, garlic, ginger, and white pepper in a pot over high heat. Add a teaspoon of salt and stir frequently, for about 5 minutes, to keep meat from sticking to bottom of cooking pot, until onions soften, and mutton starts browning and letting out its natural juice. Cover pot and let steam for 3 minutes. Turn heat off, set aside, and uncover till it cools. Then recover with lid.

3. Place fresh snails and ½ cup of water in a small pan over high heat for 5 minutes to steam snails. Save any remaining liquid.

4. In a large saucepan combine oil, red onion, ginger, garlic, Scotch Bonnet, and salt over high heat. Stir continuously for about 7–10 minutes.

5. Add tomato puree when onion bits soften and begin to turn golden brown on the edges. Continue stirring for about 2 minutes, mixing in puree.

6. Add chopped tomatoes and mix completely. Cover saucepan with lid, turn medium heat to high and let cook. After 10 minutes, add the mutton with its stock into the tomato stew. Partly cover saucepan and let stew continue to cook for 10 minutes, stirring occasionally.

7. Boil Wele with a cup water over high heat for about 10 minutes. Drain liquid afterward and discard.

8. Introduce the Wele and steamed crabs into the stew for about 2 minutes. Then add the snails with any remaining snail liquid residue and mix thoroughly into stew. Reduce heat to medium and let simmer 5 minutes. Add fish or shrimp powder and stir completely.

9. After 2 minutes, add the parboiled Okro and Garden Eggs and mix thoroughly. Break smoked mackerel and herring into bite-sized pieces and mix into stew. Partly cover the saucepan, reduce heat to low, and let simmer for 10 minutes.

10. Turn fire off. It's time to enjoy some Ghana Okro Stew with some Banku or any other cooked roots and tubers of choice.

Okro Soup

Serves: 6 | Prep Time: 15 minutes | Cooking Time: 60 minutes

Okro Soup aka telephone wire, is soup that requires skills to manoeuvre Okro in its full, slimy character glory.

The soup fully activates Okro's quality that require some twisting and turning skills developed over time to get the soup into one's mouth seemlessly. If care is not taken, you can soil your clothing.

Banku again is the preferred side for this soup.

For Soup Base

• 2 small (6oz/170g) tomatoes

• 1 small yellow onion (4oz/113g), peeled

• 2 small white Garden Eggs (4oz/113g), stems trimmed

• 2 Scotch Bonnet (Habanero) pepper

• 4oz (113g) ginger root, peeled

• 4 cloves garlic

• 2 tsp salt

• 6 cups (48fl oz/1.5L) boiling water

For Okro Mix
• 2lbs (1kg) Okro (Okra), washed, chopped fresh

For Meats/Fish
• 1lb (16oz/454g) fresh beef, clean, trimmed of excess fat, chopped to bite-size
• ½lb (8oz/227g) fresh African giant snails, de-shelled, cleaned with lemon juice
• ½lb (8oz/227g) Toolo Beefi (salt-preserved mutton), cleaned, trimmed of excess fat, cut to bite-sizes
• ½lb (8oz/227g) Wele (preserved cow hide), cleaned
• 6 live land or blue crabs or sea crabs, rinsed, steamed, legs' pointy tips broken off
• ½lb (8oz/227g) smoked mackerel, tuna, herrings, or a mix of all
• 4 cloves garlic, finely chopped
• 1 small (4oz/113g) red onion, finely chopped
• 2 tsp salt
• 2 pods Hwentia (Grains of Selim)
• 1 tsp white or black pepper
• 2 tsp minced ginger
• 2½ cups water

Preparation
1. Combine beef, red onion, garlic, ginger, Hwentia and white pepper in a large soup pot over high heat. Add a teaspoon salt and stir frequently, for about 5 minutes, to keep beef from sticking to bottom of cooking pot, until onions soften, and beef starts browning and letting out its natural juice. Cover pot and let steam for 3 minutes.

2. Clean all of the vegetables for soup base, cut Garden Eggs into quarters lengthwise, and add all to steaming beef. Add 2 cups of water, recover with lid, and let steam for about 15 minutes.

3. Meanwhile, place fresh snails and ½ cup of water in a small pan over high heat for 5 minutes to steam snails. Save any remaining liquid.

4. In a small saucepan, parboil Toolo Beefi (salt-preserved mutton) with a cup of water for 10 minutes over high heat to help reduce salt level. Set aside.

5. Also, boil Wele with 1 cup of water over high heat in another pot for about 10 minutes. Drain liquid after and discard.

6. Pick out tomatoes, onion, garlic, ginger, Scotch Bonnet and 4 quarters of Garden Egg into a blender or food processor from boiling soup base. Set aside remaining 4 quarters of Garden Egg. Add 2 cups of water to vegetables and blend completely.

7. Pour blended vegetable mix through a colander into the boiling soup base. Rinse food processor with remaining 2 cups of water and pour over any remains in colander. Discard any vegetable residue left in the colander. Mix soup base thoroughly and cover with lid to boil for 5 minutes.

8. Introduce the Wele, steamed crabs, Toolo Beefi, with 2 tablespoons of Toolo Beefi liquid residue into the soup base. After 2 minutes, add the snails with any remaining snail liquid residue and mix thoroughly. Reduce heat to medium and let soup base boil for 5 minutes.

9. Add chopped Okro and mix thoroughly into soup base. Cover with lid and continue to cook over high heat.

10. After 5 minutes break smoked mackerel, tuna and herring into bite-sized pieces and mix into soup. Partly cover the cooking pot, reduce heat to low, and let simmer for 10 minutes.

11. It's time! The Okro Soup is ready for your enjoyment. Top with remaining Garden Egg quarters for anyone interested and serve.

> **Tip: Toolo Beefi residue liquid magic**
> When more salt is needed, just add a tablespoon or two of the Tooli Beefi residue liquid.

SOUPS OF THE LAND OFTEN LAND HOT WITH JOY.

"No good soup can be rushed. If you are in a hurry, go and drink water!"

The soups from the land of Ghana often land hot in soup bowls and are now nearer to you than ever. It's right off the land to you somewhere on this globe.

The soups of the land come with their own special meat combo. The better the matched combo, the more praise for the person who made the soup. The better the variety of meats, the happier the soup participants. The better the ingredient freshness, the smiles of love and joy will abound. Don't mess up a soup or all fingers will point at you.

Right from our ancestors till now, it is imperative to remember that no good soup can be rushed. If you are in a hurry, go and drink water! The art of soup-making is serious business. Soups are made in large portions in Ghana to accommodate families and anyone who invites him or herself to the table as soon as the soup is served.

"Palm Nut Soup is so versatile at the various stages of its life cycle."
– Maame Ama

"Mm, as for that soup dierrhhh. Chale! Herrhh, e sweet ohh."
– Kofi The Soup Master

Tilapia Soup

Serves: 6

Marinade & Prep Time: 20 minutes

Cooking Time: 60 minutes

A bowl of Tilapia Soup is not a bad idea.

For Fish

• 2 large whole Tilapia, scaled, gutted, cleaned, cut into 6 pieces (3 each)

• 1 tsp salt

For Tilapia Marinade

• ½ large (5oz/142g) red onion, peeled

• 4oz (113g) ginger root, peeled

• 4 cloves garlic

• 8 Kpakpo Shito (or 2 Scotch Bonnet/1 Habanero) pepper

• 1 pod Hwentia (Grains of Selim) or 1 tsp peppercorn

• 8 tbsp (½cup/4fl oz) water

For Main Soup

• 2 medium tomatoes (½lb/8oz/227g)

• ½ large (5oz/142g) red onion, peeled

• 2oz (57g) ginger root, peeled

• 4 cloves garlic

• 1 Scotch Bonnet pepper

• 1 white Garden Egg (4oz/113g) (1 small graffiti eggplant), trimmed

• 3 pieces Okro (Okra), stems trimmed

• 1½ tsp salt

• 8 cups (64fl oz/2L) water

Preparation

1. Salt Tilapia pieces and place in a large soup pot. Combine ingredients for marinade in a blender and pour over Tilapia. Generously coat all of the pieces with blended mix. Cover pot and let marinade for 15 minutes.

2. Meanwhile, clean all vegetables and half the Garden Egg lengthwise.

3. Place soup pot with marinated Tilapia on stove top, let steam over medium heat for about 5 minutes. Fish will naturally release its juice.

4. Gently pick out steamed Tilapia pieces onto a plate and set aside. Place vegetables into Tilapia stock and add 2 cups of water, replace lid, increase heat to high and let boil for about 15 minutes.

5. Pick out all of the vegetables into a blender or food processor. Add 2 cups of water and blend completely. Pour blended vegetable mix through a colander into the boiling soup.

6. Rinse food processor with remaining water and pour over any remains in colander. Discard any vegetable residue left in the colander. Add salt, mix thoroughly, and cover with lid for soup to boil over high for 10 minutes.

7. Add Tilapia pieces, reduce heat to medium and partly cover to boil for 10 minutes. Skim fat off soup, then reduce heat to low and let simmer for 5 minutes. Turn off heat.

8. Serve your Tilapia soup as is or with your favourite side and make the best of the moment.

> **Tip: Handle with care**
> After adding fish close to the end, refrain from stirring as fish is delicate and can disintegrate. And when it's time to serve, gently pick out fish first and then scoop soup with ladle.

Ebunuebunu/Ghana Green Soup

Serves: 6 | **Prep Time:** 10 minutes | **Cooking Time:** 55 minutes

The green soup that starts with Kontomire and many say has so much heart to give at any time and keeps giving. Typical cooked with Grasscutter or Akrantie but where this bush meat is out of reach, the soup can still come alive to satisfy the soul.

For Steaming Greens

- 3 bunches (2¼lbs/36oz/1Kg) Kontomire or Taro leaves or spinach, washed, trimmed, freshly chopped
- 1 bunch (1oz/28g)/15 pieces Turkey Berry (Wild Eggplant), washed
- 14 Kpakpo Shitɔ (6 Scotch Bonnet/4 Habanero) pepper
- 12 tbsp (¾ cup/6 fl oz) water

For Main Soup

- 1 large red onion (10oz/284g), peeled
- 1 small (4oz/114g) tomato
- 3 pieces Okro (Okra), stems trimmed
- 4oz (113g) ginger root, peeled
- 8 cloves garlic
- 1 Scotch Bonnet (Habanero) pepper
- 8 cups (64fl oz/2L) water
- 1 Prekese pod, rinsed, pat dry

For Meats/Fish

- 2lbs (32oz/907g) smoked Grasscutter/Akrantie (Ghana Bush Meat/Cane Rat), chopped to bite-size, rinsed
- ½lb (8oz/227g) fresh beef, trimmed of excess fat, cleaned, cut to bite-size
- ½lb (8oz/227g) fresh African giant snails, de-shelled, cleaned with lemon juice
- 6 live land or blue crabs or sea crabs, rinsed, steamed, legs' pointy tips broken off
- ½lb (8oz/227g) smoked mudfish or Tilapia
- 1 small Koobi (salt-preserved dried Tilapia), gills removed, lightly rinsed to remove excess salt, pat dry, cut into 4-6 pieces
- 1 large red onion (10oz/284g), finely chopped
- 4 cloves garlic, finely chopped
- 2 tsp ginger, freshly minced
- 1½ tsp salt
- 9 cups (72fl oz/2.1L) water

Preparation

1. Place Grasscutter pieces and fresh beef in a large soup pot over high heat and add salt, ginger, garlic and onion. Stir occasionally for about 5–7 minutes until onion starts caramelizing. Cover pot and let steam over medium heat for about 5 minutes, stirring once or twice.

2. Meanwhile, steam Kontomire (Taro leaves), Turkey Berry and Scotch Bonnet with water in a cooking pot with a tight-fitting lid over medium heat for about 5–7 minutes. Uncover and set aside to cool.

3. Rinse tomato and Okro, place on top of steaming grasscutter. Add onion, Scotch Bonnet, garlic, ginger plus 2 cups of water. Cover soup pot with lid and let boil for 10 minutes.

4. Pick out onion, tomato, okro, Scotch Bonnet, garlic and ginger into food processor or blender. Add 2 cups of water and blend completely. Pour blended vegetable mix through a colander into the soup. Rinse food processor with 2 cups of water and pour over any remains in colander. Discard any vegetable residue left in the colander. Add Koobi and continue to boil for 5 minutes.

5. Place fresh snails and ½ cup of water in a small saucepan over high heat for 5 minutes to steam snails. Remove from fire. Save any remaining snail liquid.

6. Pour steamed green vegetables into a blender or food processor. Add 2 cups of water and blend completely. Pour blended green vegetable mix in. Rinse blender or food processor with remaining water into the soup.

7. Add steamed crabs and the snails with any remaining snail liquid residue. Mix thoroughly. Put Preskese pod over an open flame for 30 seconds to warm, break into 2 parts and add into soup as desired. Cover with lid and let soup boil for 5 minutes.

8. Reduce heat to low, uncover and stir thoroughly. Add smoked fish. Partly cover and let soup simmer for another 10–12 minutes.

9. Ebunuebunu/Ghana Green Soup, is ready! Serve this delicious soup with Fufu and spread the gift of green love.

Tip 1: Raise the temperature or not!
Add extra Kpakpo Shitɔ (Habanero) pepper to increase the pepper level or reduce the Scotch Bonnet to bring the heat level down.

Tip 2: Koobi in, salt out
Koobi's preservation with salt makes the dried fish retain most of the salt even after a light rinse with water. When Koobi goes in, salt level must be checked before adding more.

Tip 3: Steaming crabs
Carefully place live crabs into a pot, add water and salt, and cover. Place a weight on cover to prevent crabs from escaping. Steam for 10 minutes and set aside. Break off crab legs' pointy tips when they cools.

Tip 4: Other smoked meats
Replace smoked Grasscutter with other smoked meats of choice that best suits your taste.

Chicken Light Soup

Serves: 6 | **Prep Time:** 10 minutes | **Cooking Time:** 60 minutes

When a pot of Chicken Light Soup is taken off the fire in Ghana, it is considered a pot full of power. It's a light tomato base soup that's fiercely loaded with nutrients and very aromatic. Even though Ghana's Light Soup can be made with other meats, whenever it's made with chicken it revives more than one's spirit.

The ingredients that make up the soup can help anyone pick up the pace on a slow day or get some relief when the body feels a bit under the weather. Light Soup, like most soups from Ghana, is popularly eaten with Fufu, but can also be eaten as is, without a side, or paired with boiled Ghana Yam, Cocoyams, plantains, sweet potatoes, and steamed rice.

For Steaming Chicken

- 1 whole chicken
- 2 tsp salt
- 2 tsp white or black pepper
- 1½ tsp minced ginger
- 2 sprigs fresh basil
- 6 cloves garlic, finely chopped
- ½ large (5oz/142g) red onion, finely chopped

For Main Soup

- 5 medium tomatoes (1lb/½kg)
- ½ large (5oz/142g) red onion, peeled
- 2 small white Garden Eggs (4oz/113g)/1 small graffiti eggplant, trimmed
- 4 pieces Okro (Okra), stems trimmed
- 2 Scotch Bonnet (Habanero) pepper
- 4oz (113g) ginger root, peeled
- 4 cloves garlic
- 2 sprigs fresh basil
- 2½ tsp salt
- 8 cups (64fl oz/2L) water

Preparation

1. Rinse the whole chicken and cut into about 18–20 pieces. Place chicken pieces in a large soup pot over medium-high heat and add salt, white pepper, ginger, basil, garlic and onion. Stir occasionally for about 5–7 minutes until onion starts caramelizing. Cover pot and let steam over medium heat for about 10 minutes, stirring once or twice. Chicken will naturally release its juice.

2. Clean all the vegetables, halve eggplants lengthwise, and add all to steaming chicken. Add 2 cups of water, replace lid, increase heat to high, and let continue steaming for about 10 minutes.

3. Pick out all the vegetables into a blender or food processor. Add 2 cups of water and blend completely. Pour blended vegetable mix through a colander into the boiling soup.

4. Rinse food processor with remaining water and pour over any remains in colander. Discard any vegetable residue left in the colander. Add salt, mix thoroughly and cover with lid for soup to boil for 10 minutes.

5. Reduce heat to medium-low, uncover, skim fat off soup, and stir thoroughly. Partly cover, add basil, and let soup simmer for another 20–25 minutes, occasionally checking to skim fat off soup. Turn heat off.

6. The Chicken Light Soup is ready – serve and enjoy with your loved ones.

Tip 1: Mild or hot spicy option
Reduce or add more Kpakpo Shito (Scotch Bonnet) pepper to to decrease or increase the heat level of the soup.

Tip 2: Vegetarian or other meat options
Enjoy a vegetarian style by preparing the soup without chicken or any other meat. Or replace chicken with either smoked white tuna fish or beef or lamb, or combine all to suit your taste. When using smoked fish, add 30 minutes to the end as fish becomes delicate in soup and can easily disintegrate.

Tip 3: More vegetables for serving
Add 2 more small white eggplants and 4 extra pieces of Okro (Okra) into boiling soup 15 minutes before serving.

Goat Light Soup/Aponkye Nkrakra

Serves: 6 | **Prep Time:** 10 minutes | **Cooking Time:** 60 minutes

Every soup is not the same, you want the goat soup that will knock the shoes off your feet and make you want more.

Goat Light Soup is also called Aponkye Nkrakra because Aponkye is a goat in the Twi language. Ghanaians love their Goat Light Soup and will trade anything for a good and tasty bowl of this soup.

The exciting part is when it is enjoyed in a very relaxed atmosphere, it soothes the body even more. Try it after a fully loaded day of activities. Relax and enjoy!

For Steaming Goat

- 2¾lb (44oz/1.3kg) fresh goat, cleaned, trimmed of excess fat, cut to bite-sized chunks
- 1½ tsp salt
- 2 tsp white or black pepper
- 2 tsp minced ginger
- 1 pod Hwentia (Grains of Selim)
- 6 cloves garlic, finely chopped
- ½ large (5oz/142g) red onion, finely chopped

For Main Soup

- 5 medium tomatoes (1lb/½kg)
- ½ large (5oz/142g) red onion, peeled
- 2 small white Garden Eggs (4oz/113g)/1 small graffiti eggplant, trimmed
- 4 pieces Okro (Okra), stems trimmed
- 2 Scotch Bonnet (Habanero) pepper
- 4oz (113g) ginger root, peeled
- 4 cloves garlic
- 1 sprig fresh basil
- 2½ tsp salt
- 8 cups (64fl oz/2L) water

Tip 1: More vegetables for serving

Add 2 more small white eggplants and 4 extra pieces of Okro (Okra) into boiling soup 15 minutes before serving.

Tip 2: Mild or hot spicy option

Reduce or add more Kpakpo Shito (Scotch Bonnet) pepper to to decrease or increase the heat level of the soup.

Preparation

1. Place goat pieces in a large soup pot over high heat and add salt, white pepper, Hwentia, ginger, garlic and onion. Stir occasionally for about 5–7 minutes until onion starts caramelizing. Cover pot and let steam over medium heat for about 10 minutes, stirring once or twice. Goat meat will naturally release its juice.

2. Clean all the vegetables, half eggplants lengthwise, and add all to steaming chicken. Add 2 cup of water, replace lid, increase heat to high and let steam for about 10 minutes.

3. Pick out all the vegetables into a blender or food processor. Add 2 cups of water and blend completely. Pour blended vegetable mix through a colander into the boiling soup.

4. Rinse food processor with remaining water and pour over any remains in colander. Discard any vegetable residue left in the colander. Add salt, mix thoroughly and cover with lid for soup to boil for 10 minutes.

5. Reduce heat to medium, uncover, skim fat off soup and stir thoroughly. Partly cover, add basil and let soup simmer for another 20–25 minutes, occasionally checking to skim fat off soup. Turn heat off.

6. It's time for some Goat Light Soup. Enjoy the soup with fufu or something else.

Tip 3: Vegetarian or other meat options

Enjoy a vegetarian style by preparing the soup without chicken or any other meat. Or replace chicken with either smoked white tuna fish or beef or lamb, or combine all to suit your taste. When using smoked fish, add 30 minutes to the end as fish becomes delicate in soup and can easily disintegrate.

Groundnut Soup With Chicken

Serves: 6 | **Prep Time:** 15 minutes | **Cooking Time:** 100 minutes

Some say groundnuts are peanuts, but we say it's nuts from the ground, so groundnuts. The one soup I repeatedly hear of from numerous individuals who have had the opportunity to visit Ghana is the almighty Groundnut Soup. This soup of the land is so delicious and among the top ones on the charts. It might be difficult to come to terms with what you hear until you actually come to terms with a bowl of Groundnut Soup.

As our mothers and grandmothers say in Ghana, "No good soup can be rushed." Groundnut Soup is one special soup that needs all the nurturing to get the best out of it. From the groundnut selection to the type of meat, it's important to invest time, maximum effort, and care to produce the best in class soup. Now nurture your own pot of Groundnut Soup from this recipe and enjoy a Ghanaian classic.

For Cooking Groundnut Paste (Peanut Butter)

• 16oz (454grams) groundnut paste (or creamy peanut butter)
• 6 cups (48fl oz/1.5L) hot water

For Steaming Chicken

• 1 whole chicken
• 2 tsp salt
• 2 tsp white or black pepper
• 2½ tsp ginger, freshly minced
• 2 sprigs fresh basil
• 6 cloves garlic, finely chopped
• ½ large (5oz/142g) red onion, finely chopped

For Main Soup

- 5 medium tomatoes (1lb/½kg)
- ½ large (5oz/142g) red onion, peeled
- 2 small white Garden Eggs (4oz/113g)/1 small graffiti eggplant, trimmed
- 4 pieces Okro (Okra), stems trimmed
- 2 Scotch Bonnet (Habanero) pepper
- 4oz (113g) ginger root, peeled, halved
- 4 cloves garlic
- 1 tbsp salt
- 8 cups (64fl oz/2L) water

Preparation

1. In a large soup pot, mix groundnut paste thoroughly with hot water. Let boil over high heat for about 15 minutes, stirring occasionally with a wooden spoon.

2. Meanwhile, rinse the whole chicken and cut into about 18–20 pieces. Place chicken pieces in another cooking pot over high heat and add salt, white pepper, ginger, basil, garlic and finely chopped onion. Stir occasionally for about 5–7 minutes until onion starts caramelizing. Then cover pot and let steam over medium heat for about 10 minutes, occasionally stirring. Turn heat off.

3. Reduce heat of boiling groundnut mix to low. Let boil for 15–20 minutes more until it starts simmering and oil rises to the top. Skim off groundnut oil. This is pure groundnut oil you can save for another dish.

4. Add steamed chicken with all the broth or stock to the groundnut mix. Use 2 cups of water to rinse steamed chicken pot of any remaining residue and add to the groundnut soup mix.

5. Add 2 more cups of water. Mix thoroughly and let groundnut mix boil over high heat. Rinse the vegetables. Halve eggplant lengthwise, add together with whole tomatoes, onion, Scotch Bonnet, garlic, ginger, and Okro (Okra) to boiling soup. Cover soup pot with lid and let boil for 15 minutes.

6. Pick out all the vegetables into a food processor or blender. Add 2 cups of water and blend completely. Pour blended vegetable mix through a colander into the boiling soup.

7. Rinse food processor with remaining 2 cups of water and pour over any remains in the colander into soup. Discard any vegetable residue left in the colander. Add salt, mix thoroughly, and cover with lid for soup to boil for 10 minutes.

8. Reduce heat to low, uncover, skim fat off soup, and stir thoroughly. Partly cover and let soup simmer for another 25 minutes, occasionally checking to skim fat off soup. Turn heat off.

9. It's time to serve this delicious soup and share with loved ones.

> **Tip 1: Mild or hot spicy option**
> Reduce or add more Kpakpo Shitɔ (Scotch Bonnet) pepper to to decrease or increase the heat level of the soup.

> **Tip 2: Use chicken breeds or poultry varieties better suited for soups**
> In Ghana, chicken breeds or poultry varieties that are free range and lay eggs are commonly used for soups in order to keep the cut chicken pieces more intact by the time the soup is ready. The breeds used for roasting easily disintegrate into bits by the time the soup is cooked.

> **Tip 3: More vegetables for serving**
> Add 2 more small white eggplants and 4 extra pieces of Okro (Okra) into boiling soup 15 minutes before serving.

Groundnut Soup With Meat Varieties

Serves: 6 | **Prep Time:** 20 minutes | **Cooking Time:** 100 minutes

For Steaming Meats
- 1lb (16oz/454g) fresh beef, trimmed of excess fat, cleaned, cut to bite-size
- ½lb (8oz/227g) fresh tripe, cleaned
- ½lb (8oz/227g) mutton, trimmed of excess fat, cleaned
- 6 cloves garlic, finely chopped
- ½ large (5oz/142g) red onion, finely chopped
- 1½ tsp salt
- 1½ tsp white or black pepper
- 2 pods Hwentia (Grains of Selim)
- 2 tsp ginger, freshly minced

For African Giant Snails
- ½lb (8oz/227g) fresh African giant snails, de-shelled, cleaned with lemon juice
- 8 tbsp (½ cup/4oz) water

For Land Crabs
- 6 live land or blue crabs
- 2 cups (16fl oz/474ml) water
- ½ tsp salt

For Smoked Fish
- ½lb (8oz/227g) smoked mackerel, tuna, herrings, or a mix of all

For Main Soup
- 5 medium tomatoes (1lb/½kg)
- ½ large (5oz/142g) red onion, peeled
- 2 small white Garden Eggs (4oz/113g)/1 small graffiti eggplant, trimmed
- 4 pieces Okro (Okra), stems trimmed
- 7 Kpakpo Shito (4 Scotch Bonnet /3 Habanero) pepper
- 4oz (113g) ginger root, peeled, halved
- 4 cloves garlic
- 1 tbsp salt
- 9 cups (72fl oz/2.1L) water

Preparation

1. In a large soup pot, mix groundnut paste thoroughly with hot water. Let boil over high heat for about 15 minutes, stirring occasionally with a wooden spoon.

2. Meanwhile, combine beef, tripe, mutton, red onion, garlic, ginger, salt, black pepper and Grains of Selim another cooking pot over high heat. Stir occasionally for about 5–7 minutes until onion starts caramelizing. Then cover pot and let steam over medium heat for about 10 minutes, occasionally stirring. Turn heat off.

3. Place fresh de-shelled snails and ½ cup of water in a small cooking pot over high heat for 5 minutes to steam snails. Save any remaining liquid.

4. Reduce heat of boiling groundnut mix to low. Let boil for 15–20 minutes more until it starts simmering and oil rises to the top. Skim off groundnut oil. This is pure groundnut oil you can save for another dish.

5. Add steamed beef, tripe and mutton with all the broth or stock to the groundnut mix. Use 2 cups of water to rinse steamed pot of any remaining residue and add to the groundnut soup mix.

6. Add 2 more cups of water. Mix thoroughly and let groundnut mix boil over high heat. Rinse the vegetables. Halve eggplant lengthwise, add together with whole tomatoes, onion, Scotch Bonnet, garlic, ginger, and Okro to boiling soup. Cover soup pot with lid and let boil for 15 minutes.

7. Carefully place live crabs into a pot, add water and salt, and cover. Place a weight on cover to prevent the crabs from escaping. Steam for 10 minutes, set aside.

8. Pick out all the vegetables into a blender. Add 2 cups of water and blend completely. Pour blended vegetable mix through a colander into the boiling soup.

9. Rinse food processor with remaining 3 cups of water and pour over any remains in the colander into soup. Discard any vegetable residue left in the colander. Break off steamed crab legs' pointy tips and add. Add the snails with any remaining snail liquid residue. Mix thoroughly, add salt, and cover with lid. Let soup to boil for 10 minutes.

10. Reduce heat to low, uncover, skim fat off soup and stir thoroughly. Add smoked fish. Partly cover and let soup simmer for another 25 minutes, occasionally checking to skim fat off soup. Turn heat off.

11. It's time to serve this delicious pot of goodness and share with your loved ones.

> **Tip 1: Mild or hot spicy option**
> Reduce or add more Kpakpo Shitɔ (Scotch Bonnet) pepper to to decrease or increase the heat level of the soup.

> **Tip 2: More vegetables for serving**
> Add 2 more small white eggplants and 4 extra pieces of Okro (Okra) into boiling soup 15 minutes before serving.

> **Tip 3: Add and subtract meats per preference**
> Add or subtract, beef, mutton, tripe, and cow trotters per preference or combine with smoked white tuna fish or smoked mackerel to suit your taste. When using smoked fish, add 30 minutes to the end as fish becomes delicate in soup and can easily disintegrate.

Palm Nut Soup/Abenkwan

Serves: 6 | Prep Time: 20 minutes | Cooking Time: 100 minutes

A good selection of palm fruits produces the Palm Nut Soup of your dreams.

A big cluster or bunch of palm fruits is cut from the palm tree before it is separated traditionally by hand from its natural prickly resting pockets. Care must be taken when removing the individual fruits because one can easily get pricked a few times. Palm fruits that are bad are removed from the collection. The individual fruits are rinsed a few times and then boiled in water.

Once cooked, the water is drained, and the fruits get pounded in a large mortar with pestle. This traditional method rips the fleshy fruity skin from the nuts. Hot water is added when the fruit flesh is separated from the nuts. Then, it is poured through large colanders to extract palm fruit concentrate to form the base for the soup. The nuts are then separated from the fibre remains in the colander for deshelling and onwards production of palm kernel oil.

Palm Nut Soup should clearly be called Palm Fruit Soup as the palm soup base comes from the fruits and not the nuts, but most people argue that the former sounds better. Some are leaning to Palm Soup and call it that.

Nowadays, the traditional labour-intensive extraction process has evolved, and the soup base is widely available in caned form to help save some time. There's no excuse now to not cook Palm Nut Soup for the family.

For Soup Vegetables
- 5 medium tomatoes (1lb/½kg)
- 1 large red onion (10oz/284g), peeled
- 3 small white Garden Eggs (4oz/113g)/2 small graffiti eggplant, trimmed
- 6 pieces Okro (Okra), stems trimmed
- 4 Scotch Bonnet (2 Habanero) pepper
- 4oz (113g) ginger root, peeled, halved
- 10 cloves garlic
- 1 tbsp salt
- 9 cups (72fl oz/2.1L) water

For Palm Base
- 28oz (780grams) canned Palm Soup Base
- 8 cups (64fl oz/2L) hot water

For Nane (Salt-Preserved Pig Feet)
- ¾lb (12oz/340g) salted pig feet, cleaned, cut to small chunks
- 2 cups (16fl oz/474ml) water

For Land Crabs
- 6 live land or blue crabs
- 2 cups water
- ½ tsp salt

For Smoked Fish
- 1lb (16oz//½kg) smoked tuna

For Steaming Meats
- 1lb (16oz/454g) fresh beef, cleaned, trimmed of excess fat, bite-sized cuts
- ½lb (8oz/227g) mutton, cleaned, trimmed of excess fat, bite-sized cuts
- ½lb (8oz/227g) fresh tripe, cleaned
- ½lb (8oz/227g) cow trotters, cleaned, cut to small chunks
- 6 cloves garlic, finely chopped
- 1 large red onion (10oz/284g), finely chopped
- 2 tsp salt
- 8 pieces Kpakpo Shito (or 2 Scotch Bonnet) pepper, finely chopped
- 1 tsp white or black pepper
- 3 tsp ginger, freshly minced

Preparation

1. Put Nane (salt-preserved pig feet) pieces in cooking pot with 2 cups of water over medium-high to boil for 20 minutes and set aside.

2. Meanwhile, combine beef, mutton, tripe, cow trotters, red onion, garlic, ginger, salt, Kpakpo Shito, white pepper and Hwentia in a large soup pot over high heat. Stir occasionally for about 7–10 minutes until onion starts caramelizing. Cover pot with lid and let steam over medium heat for about 10 more minutes, occasionally stirring.

3. Rinse vegetables, halve Garden Eggs lengthwise, add, plus whole tomatoes, whole peeled onion, Scotch Bonnet, garlic, ginger, Okra to steaming meats. Add 4 cups water. Cover and boil for 15 minutes.

4. Carefully place live crabs into a pot, add water and salt, and cover. Place a weight on cover to prevent crabs from escaping. Steam for 10 minutes and set aside. Break off crab legs' pointy tips when they cools.

5. Pick out all the vegetables into a food processor or blender. Add 3 cups of water and blend completely. Pour blended vegetable mix through a colander into the boiling soup base.

6. Rinse food processor with remaining 2 cups of water and pour over any remains in the colander into soup. Discard any vegetable residue left in the colander. Add Nane, mix thoroughly, and cover with lid. Let to boil for 10 minutes.

7. Open canned palm soup base, add and stir completely to mix. Gently drop in the steamed crabs and 6 cups of hot water. Mix thoroughly and cover with lid for soup to continue boiling.

8. After 10 minutes, reduce heat to medium-low, uncover, skim fat off soup and stir thoroughly. Add smoked fish. Partly cover and let soup simmer for another 20 minutes, occasionally checking to skim oil off soup. Taste to check salt level. A tablespoon or two of Nane liquid residue can be added, as it contains salt for desired taste.

9. Stir soup one last time and reduce heat to low for 5–10 minutes for final simmering and thickening to desired fluidity. The soup is ready for you!

Akplijii/Kaaweku/Aprapransa

Serves: 6 | Prep Time: 10 minutes | Cooking Time: 145 minutes

In loving memory of the late Kate OKailey Brenya, who styled this recipe.

From Ada, the land known for Ghana's Land Crabs, comes a very special dish. With Ga-Adangbe roots, this dish is cooked for royal events such as the celebration of new royals including chiefs and queen mothers, as well as for festivals and other special occasions. This dish has made headway into kitchens and homes across Ghana because it tastes so good. At family gatherings, parties, and events, it's one of the first dishes that vanishes if you blink.

During the '90s, this dish received national attention when it was featured in a TV comedy series with Ghanaian actor Idikoko (Augustine Abbey), entrusted to deliver Aprapransa to his employer, Mr. Amstrong (the late actor Mac Jordan Amartey) by Mrs. Amstrong. While on the errand, the Aprapransa aroma got to Idikoko and he succumbed and devoured Mr. Amstrong's lunch. That comedic scene propelled many who were yet to try Aprapransa to immediately act and try the dish.

It's an open secret that if you want the best Akplijii or Kaaweku or Aprapransa, you marry a Ga-Adangbe woman, and some will specifically point you to Ada as your starting location because the natives of Ada know how to prepare crab-related dishes and Ga-Adangbes are skillful in Palm Nut Soup preparation. Crabs, called Kaa in Ga language and Kaawe in the Dangbe language, is very prominent in this meal.

The royalness of this meal deserves all of the respect and attention to detail in preparing it from start to finish. Often two or three women prepare it as they happily chat and work their way through the cooking process. It is a gradual process. Do not attempt if you do not have the patience.

Now it's your turn to attempt to be in the royal courts.

For Warming Smoked Herring

• ¾lb (12oz/340g) smoked herring, skin removed, lighly rinsed, pat dry, broken to piece
• 1 large (10oz/284g) red onion, finely chopped
• 2 tsp salt
• 8 pieces Kpakpo Shitɔ (or 2 Scotch Bonnet) pepper, finely chopped
• 6 cloves garlic, finely chopped
• 3 tsp ginger, freshly minced
• 4 tbsp water

For Land Crabs

• 6 live land or blue crabs
• 2 cups (16fl oz/474ml) water
• ½ tsp salt

For Roasted Corn Flour

• 9 cups (40oz/1.1Kg) roasted corn flour

For Palm Base

• 28oz (780grams) canned Palm Soup Base
• 8 cups (64fl oz/2L) hot water

For Palm Soup Vegetables

• 5 medium tomatoes (1lb/½kg)
• 1 large (10oz/284g) red onion, peeled
• 3 small white Garden Eggs (4oz/113g)/2 small graffiti eggplant trimmed
• 6 pieces Okro (Okra), stems trimmed
• 4 Scotch Bonnet (2 Habanero) pepper
• 4oz (113g) ginger root, peeled, halved
• 10 cloves garlic
• 1 tbsp salt
• 9 cups (72fl oz/2.1L) water

For Tomato Gravy Topping

• 8 medium tomatoes (2lbs/1kg), chopped
• 1 large yellow onion (10oz/284g), chopped, onion ring quarters
• 8 pieces Kpakpo Shitɔ (2 Scotch Bonnet) pepper, finely chopped
• 4 cloves garlic, finely chopped
• 2 tsp ginger, freshly minced
• 1 tsp dried shrimp powder (dried fish powder)
• 10 tbsp (5fl oz/148ml) vegetable oil
• 1 tsp tomato puree (or paste)
• 1½ tsp salt

For Precooked Beans

• 1 cup (8oz/227g) precooked black eye beans or red beans

Preparation

1. Combine herring pieces, red onion, garlic, ginger, Kpakpo Shitɔ, and salt in a large soup pot over high heat. Stir occasionally for 5 minutes as onion starts caramelizing. Add 4 tablespoons of water and cover pot with lid and let's steam for 5 more minutes.

2. Open canned palm soup base, add together with 8 cups of water into soup pot and stir completely to mix with herring pieces. Replace lid and let cook for about 10 minutes over high.

3. Meanwhile, carefully place live crabs into another pot, add water, salt, and cover. Place a weight on cover to prevent crabs from escaping. Steam for 10 minutes and set aside. Break off crab legs' pointy tips when it cools.

4. Rinse the vegetables. Give the soup base a good stir. Halve Garden Eggs lengthwise, add, plus whole tomatoes, whole peeled onion, Scotch Bonnet, garlic, ginger, okra to boiling soup base. Add 4 cups water, cover soup pot with lid and let continue to boil for 15 minutes.

5. Pick out all the vegetables into food processor or blender. Add 3 cups of water and blend completely. Pour blended vegetable mix through a colander into the boiling soup base.

6. Rinse food processor with remaining 2 cups of water and pour over any remains in the colander into soup. Discard any vegetable residue left in the colander. Add salt and mix thoroughly and cover with lid to boil for 10 minutes.

7. Gently drop in the steamed crabs and precooked beans. Mix thoroughly and cover with lid for soup to continue boiling.

8. After 10 minutes, reduce heat to medium low, uncover, skim fat off soup and stir thoroughly. Taste to check salt level and adjust accordingly. Partly cover and let soup simmer for another 15 minutes, occasionally checking to skim oil off soup.

9. Jump onto, to prepare the Tomato Gravy topping. Grab a saucepan, combine oil, yellow onion, ginger, garlic, Kpakpo Shitɔ (Scotch Bonnet) and salt over high heat for about 5–7 minutes, stirring continuously.

10. Add tomato puree to sizzling onion mix when onion soften and begin to turn golden brown on the edges. Continue stirring for 2 minutes, mixing in puree.

11. Add chopped tomatoes and mix completely. Cover saucepan with lid and let cook for about 10 minutes. Then reduce heat to medium and tip lid slightly so saucepan is partly covered to allow some steam to escape.

12. Check on soup and give it a good stir. Take another cooking pot and with a soup ladle scoop about 40% of Palm Nut Soup to set aside.

13. Jump right back to Tomato Stew saucepan and add the teaspoon of dried shrimp or dried fish powder. Now, lower the stew to lowest temperature and let it simmer for 5–10 minutes depending on how thick you prefer the stew. Then, turn heat off.

14. Now to the main event of making the Akplijii or Aprapransa, grab a Gigintso or Banku Ta (Banku-Making Wooden Stick).

Alternatively, a large wooden spoon can be utilized in the absence of a Gigintso.

15. Reduce Palm Nut Soup heat to low. Scoop out crabs onto a plate and set aside.

16. Using a ladle, gradually add the roasted corn flour into the soup and stir with Gigintso. It is a very gradual process of adding roasted corn flour and stirring into a lump free mixture. Stir and knead to the side of the soup pot, then add more roasted corn flour. Repeat the process till all the roasted corn flour is used. Continue kneading for a lump free mixture for about 10 minutes.

17. Increase the heat to medium. Add more Palm Nut Soup, ladle by ladle from the 40% set aside as the roasted corn flour absorbs the soup quickly. The mixture should be fluid for the Gigintso (wooden spoon) to be able to move in a free motion. Do not make it dense as Akplijii or Aprapransa will set in the end. Add more soup as needed and continue kneading for 10 more minutes into a lump free paste similar to mashed potatoes.

18. Reduce the heat to low again and knead a few more times for 5 minutes, add more soup if needed to make it less dense and a little more fluid.

19. Turn the heat off and pour the mix into a favourite glass serving ware or pan of choice. Using a spoon, smoothen the surface and arrange the crabs on top of it and finally top with some Tomato Gravy. Cover and let it set for 5 minutes.

20. Time to dig in and enjoy this wonderful dish.

Tip 1: Please take your time
This is one special recipe that takes time especially once the roasted corn flour is added into the soup, please take your time.

Tip 2: Mild or spicy Tomato Gravy topping option
Reduce or add more Kpakpo Shitɔ (Scotch Bonnet/Habanero) to increase the pepper heat level from a mild to hot.

Tip 3: Smoked Mackerel in Tomato Gravy
Some people like a more joy to the Tomato Gravy so smoked mackerel is added. Remove mackerel bones and break into bite sizes and add to gravy about 2 minutes before taking the stew off the fire.

Tip 4: Extra beans
Add extra precooked on the side when serving for all who love extra beans in their Akplijii or Kaaweku or Aprapransa.

Gigintso (Ga) | Banku Ta (Twi)

Roasted Corn Flour (Abelemamu)

Kpotonkpoto/Mpotompoto/Pottage

Serves: 4 | **Prep Time:** 10 minutes | **Cooking Time:** 50 minutes

For Cooking Roots & Tubers

- ¼ tuber (1lbs/454g) Ghana Yam (West African Yam), peeled, cut to 1-inch cubes
- 1lbs (454g) Cocoyam (Taro), peeled, cut to 1-inch cubes
- 3 sweet potato (24oz/680g), peeled, cut to 1-inch cubes
- 4½ cups (36oz/1L) water
- 2 tsp salt

For Main Part

- 2 large tomatoes (1lb/454g), cleaned
- ½ large (5oz/142g) yellow onion, peeled
- 8 Kpakpo Shitɔ (or 2 Scotch Bonnet/1 Habanero) pepper
- 4 cloves garlic, finely chopped
- 2 tsp ginger, freshly minced
- 1 tsp tomato puree (or paste)
- 2 tsp dried shrimp powder
- 4 cups (32fl oz/1L) water

For Zomi Ending

- 4 tbsp (2fl oz/60ml) Zomi (spiced palm oil)
- ½ large (5oz/142g) yellow onion, finely chopped
- 1 tsp salt
- ¼lb (4oz/113g) smoked herrings, skin peeled, broken into pieces

Preparation

1. Bring to boil roots variety of Ghana Yam, cocoyam, sweet potatoes, water, and salt in a large soup pot over medium-high heat. Cover with lid and let cook for about 15 minutes.

2. Meanwhile, warm Zomi in a saucepan over medium heat. Add chopped onion and ½ teaspoon salt. Stir continuously for about 5 minutes. As onion bits soften, add smoked herring pieces, and stir for another 3 minutes. Remove from fire and set aside.

3. Uncover soup pot and place tomatoes, half onion, Kpapkp Shitɔ, garlic and ginger on top of boiling roots. Replace lid and let continue boiling.

4. After 15 minutes, reduce heat to medium and pick out tomatoes, onion, Kpapkp Shitɔ, garlic and ginger into a blender or food processor. Add 2 cups of water and blend completely. Pour blended vegetable mix through a colander onto the boiling cubed roots variety.

5. Rinse food processor with remaining water and pour over any remains in colander. Discard any vegetable residue left in the colander. Add tomato paste. Mix thoroughly and cover with lid boil for 5 minutes.

6. Add shrimp powder and mix completely. Pick out a ladle or two full for cubed roots variety into clay-grinding bowl (Asanka) with wooden masher and mash into a paste or use a food processor.

7. Add mashed roots vegetable paste and mix thoroughly. This mashed paste mix will act as a thickener.

8. Pour the Zomi and herring pieces on top of boiling roots variety and mix thoroughly. Taste for salt.

9. Let simmer for 10 minutes over low heat, stirring occasionally.

10. It is ready to eat! Serve this pot of Kpotonkpoto or Mpotompoto.

> **Tip: Mild or hot spicy option**
> Reduce or add more Kpakpo Shitɔ (Scotch Bonnet) pepper to increase the pepper heat level to hot or keep it mild.

BREAKFAST – GH STYLE

Hausa Koko
(Millet Porridge)

Ghana (Gh) has some exciting breakfast items that are tasty. We love our porridges and pairing partners of mostly different breads, but also Koose, Bofrot, and Toogbei. Here's some of the popular options easily found around town.

Oblaayo
(Corn Hominy)

Tom Brown
(Roasted Corn Porridge)

Ma Koko
(Corn Porridge)

Brodo Kɛ Paya
Bread & Avocado Pear

Koose
(Egg Included Version)

Rice Water

Ghana Sugar Bread

Koose
(Pure Beans Version)

THE GHANA TOMATO BRIGADE, ITS SIBLINGS & OFFSPRING

Tomatoes plays a major role in Ghana and are in a majority of stews and soups. For most Ghanaian stews, tomatoes are combined with onions, peppers, garlic, ginger, and other spices into a delicious meal. It's a teamwork and pure chemistry that brings great achievements to numerous cooking pots all over plus happiness to the doorsteps of many families. How the ingredients in the rank and file are combined matters a lot especially with onion cuts and colours. Should you want more sweetness, combine a mix of yellow and red onions in a stew. For sweetness and a bit of oomph, mix yellow, red, and spring onions. For tomatoes, when chopped, it cooks faster than when blended. Welcome to the brigade and enjoy yourself.

Finely chopped

Chopped

Chopped, onion ring quarters

Sliced

Blended

Sliced, onion ring style

Fish Stew

Serves: 6

Prep Time: 10 minutes

Cooking Time: 45 minutes

For anytime of the day or the week, or the month, Fish Stew delivers!

For Fish

• 1 large Grouper or Red Snapper or Whiting, scaled, gutted, cleaned, cut into 8–10 pieces

• 2 tsp ginger, freshly minced

• 1 tsp salt

• 5 tsp flour

For Frying

• 12 tbsp (6fl oz/177ml) vegetable oil

For Stew

• 8 medium tomatoes (2lbs/1kg)

• 1 large red onion (10oz/284g), thinly sliced

• 3 Scotch Bonnet (2 Habanero) pepper, finely chopped

• 5 cloves garlic, finely chopped

• 2½ tsp ginger, freshly minced

• 10 tbsp (5fl oz/148ml) vegetable oil

• 1½ tsp salt

• 2 tsp tomato puree (or paste)

> **Tip 1: Raise the temperature!**
> Add extra Scotch Bonnet (Habanero) pepper to increase the pepper heat level or reduce the Scotch Bonnet to bring the heat level down.

Preparation

1. Grab a saucepan, and heat oil over medium heat. Salt fish, spice with ginger and dust lightly with flour on all sides.

2. Once the oil is hot, fry fish in batches by placing in oil for 2–3 minutes on each side, until golden brown. Flip and repeat. Be careful as oil may splatter. Use a splatter screen for protection. Set fried fish aside on a plate lined with kitchen paper or paper towel.

3. Begin the stew by adding red onion, ginger, garlic, Scotch Bonnet and salt into the oil for about 5–7 minutes once last batch of fish is out. Stir continuously.

> **Tip 2: Fry fish without flour**
> You are at liberty to fry the fish pieces without coating with flour.

4. Add tomato puree to sizzling onion mix when onion bits soften and begin to turn golden brown on the edges. Continue stirring for about 2 minutes, mixing in puree.

5. Meanwhile, cut tomatoes into quarters and blend in a food processor or blender.

6. Add blended tomatoes and mix completely. Cover saucepan with lid and let cook.

7. After 10 minutes reduce heat to medium and tip lid slightly to partly cover saucepan to allow some steam to escape. Let stew continue to cook for 15 minutes, stirring occasionally.

8. Reduce heat to low, add fried fish pieces and let simmer for 5 more minutes. Turn heat off, grab a plate, and partake in the fish stew.

Fante Fante

Serves: 6 | Prep Time: 10 minutes | Cooking Time: 35 minutes

The stew called Fante Fante is a coastal gem that traces its roots to the Fante people of Ghana. It is made by cooking fresh fish in a tomato stew with palm oil base and simmered into a delicious dish that's capable of changing one's mood to pure joy. Cape Coast, a coastal city and the capital of the Central Region of Ghana, is believed to be where the stew gained its popularity before spreading far and wide throughout the country.

It's a fisherman's dish that is a simple "crowd-puller" and made either on canoes by fishermen using some of their fresh catch or right upon returning to land to enjoy with families. Many years later, another variation has joined the Fante Fante league. In this alternate version, the fish is partially grilled for a few seconds to help keep the fish from disintegrating in the stew. Nevertheless, the original version always wears the crown. Whiting and Longfin Herring were tradionally used for Fante Fante. These days, Red Fish (Red Snapper) and Tilapia are popular in the dish too, as well as other fishes of choice.

For Fish
- 1 large Tilapia or Red Snapper or Whiting or Mackerel, scaled, gutted, cleaned, cut into 6 pieces
- 1½ tsp salt

For Stew
- 9 tbsp (4½fl oz/133ml) palm oil
- 3 large tomatoes (2lbs/1kg), chopped
- 1 medium yellow onion (8oz/227g), chopped, onion ring quarters
- 3 Scotch Bonnet (2 Habanero) pepper, finely chopped
- 4 cloves garlic, finely chopped
- 5 tsp ginger, freshly minced
- 1 tsp salt
- 2 tsp tomato puree (or paste)

Preparation

1. In a large saucepan, warm palm oil over medium heat. Add Scotch Bonnet, yellow onion, garlic, ginger and salt into palm oil. Stir continuously for about 7–10 minutes.

2. Add tomato puree when onion bits soften and begin to turn golden brown on the edges. Continue stirring for about 2 minutes, mixing in puree.

3. Add chopped tomatoes and mix completely. Cover saucepan with lid, turn heat to medium-high and let cook.

4. Meanwhile, salt fresh fish pieces and set aside on a plate.

5. Add fresh fish pieces after 8 minutes. Partly cover saucepan and continue to cook for 7 minutes, stirring occasionally. Flip fish at least once during this period.

6. Reduce heat to the lowest and let simmer for 5 minutes.

7. Oh yes, it's ready to be served! Have a blast with this coastal Ghana fisher folk favourite.

> **Tip 1: Partially grill fish to help keep the fish from easily disintegrating**
> Alternatively, after adding tomatoes, salt fish and partially grill fish pieces over medium, a minute on each side – long enough for grill marks to begin its appearance on fish skin. Remove from grill and set aside on a plate to add to stew.

> **Tip 2: Raise the temperature or not!**
> Add extra Scotch Bonnet (Habanero) pepper to increase the pepper heat level or reduce the Scotch Bonnet to bring the heat level down.

Koobi Flɔ/Koobi Stew

Serves: 6 | Prep Time: 10 minutes | Cooking Time: 45 minutes

For Koobi
• 2 medium Koobi (salt-preserved dried Tilapia), gills removed, lightly rinsed to remove excess salt, pat dry, cut into 6 pieces

For Eggs
• 6 free range eggs

For Stew
• 8 medium tomatoes (2lbs/1kg), chopped
• 1 large yellow onion (10oz/284g), sliced, onion rings style
8 pieces Kpakpo Shitɔ (2 Scotch Bonnet) pepper, finely chopped
• 4 cloves garlic, finely chopped
• 2 tsp ginger, freshly minced
• 10 tbsp (5fl oz/148ml) vegetable oil
• 1 tsp tomato puree (or paste)

Koobi Flɔ (say "flor") or Koobi Stew is another coastal gem, a treasure from the Ga-Adangbe and a salute to all the departed souls of grandmothers in the Ga communities who made sure that Koobi Flɔ lived on till now for more and more generations to enjoy such a treasured pot of goodness. It's a treasure in a cooking pot for all to enjoy.

Preparation

1. Grab a saucepan and heat oil over medium heat. Once the oil is hot, fry Koobi pieces by placing in oil for 3–4 minutes on each side. Flip and repeat. Be careful as oil might splatter. Use a splatter screen for protection. Set Koobi pieces aside on a plate.

2. Begin the stew by adding yellow onion, ginger, garlic and Scotch Bonnet into the oil for about 5–7 minutes once Koobi pieces are out. Stir continuously.

3. Add tomato puree to sizzling onion mix when onion rings soften and begin to turn golden brown on the edges. Continue stirring for about 2 minutes, mixing in puree.

4. Meanwhile, cut tomatoes into quarters and blend in a food processor or blender.

5. Add chopped tomatoes and mix completely. Cover saucepan with lid and let cook.

6. After 10 minutes reduce heat to medium and tip lid slightly to partly cover saucepan to allow some steam to escape. Let stew continue to cook for 5 minutes, stirring occasionally.

7. Reach for the eggs. Crack egg one after the other and gently drop into the stew, making sure to space eggs evenly in the stew. Do not stir. Cover with lid.

8. After 3 minutes flip the eggs. Again, do not stir stew. Cover for 2 more minutes as the eggs cook and each take on its own beautiful individual imperfect circular shape.

9. Reduce heat to low, add fried Koobi pieces by gently using a spoon to create spaces between the eggs. Partly cover with lid and let simmer for 5 more minutes. Turn heat off, the Koobi Stew is ready to enjoy and put smiles on any nearby hungry face.

Tip 1: Ga Tomato Gravy?
You might have heard and might want to try a Ga Tomata Gravy. Follow the same preparation steps but omit the Koobi and eggs. Ga Tomato Gravy goes well with Kenkey and fried fish.

Tip 2: No salt please! Koobi is salt-preserved dried Tilapia!
The way Koobi is preserved with salt makes the dried fish retain most of the salt even after a light rinse with water. Koobi stew is a stew made without salt because Koobi contains enough salt.

Tip 3: Raise the temperature or not!
Add extra Scotch Bonnet (Habanero) pepper to increase the pepper heat level or reduce the Scotch Bonnet to bring the heat level down.

Tip 4: Omit the eggs
Koobi is known for its appeal with eggs but feel free to not add eggs and in the process save some time too.

Tip 5: Chop tomatoes easily!
Use a serrated or bread knife to chop tomatoes easily.

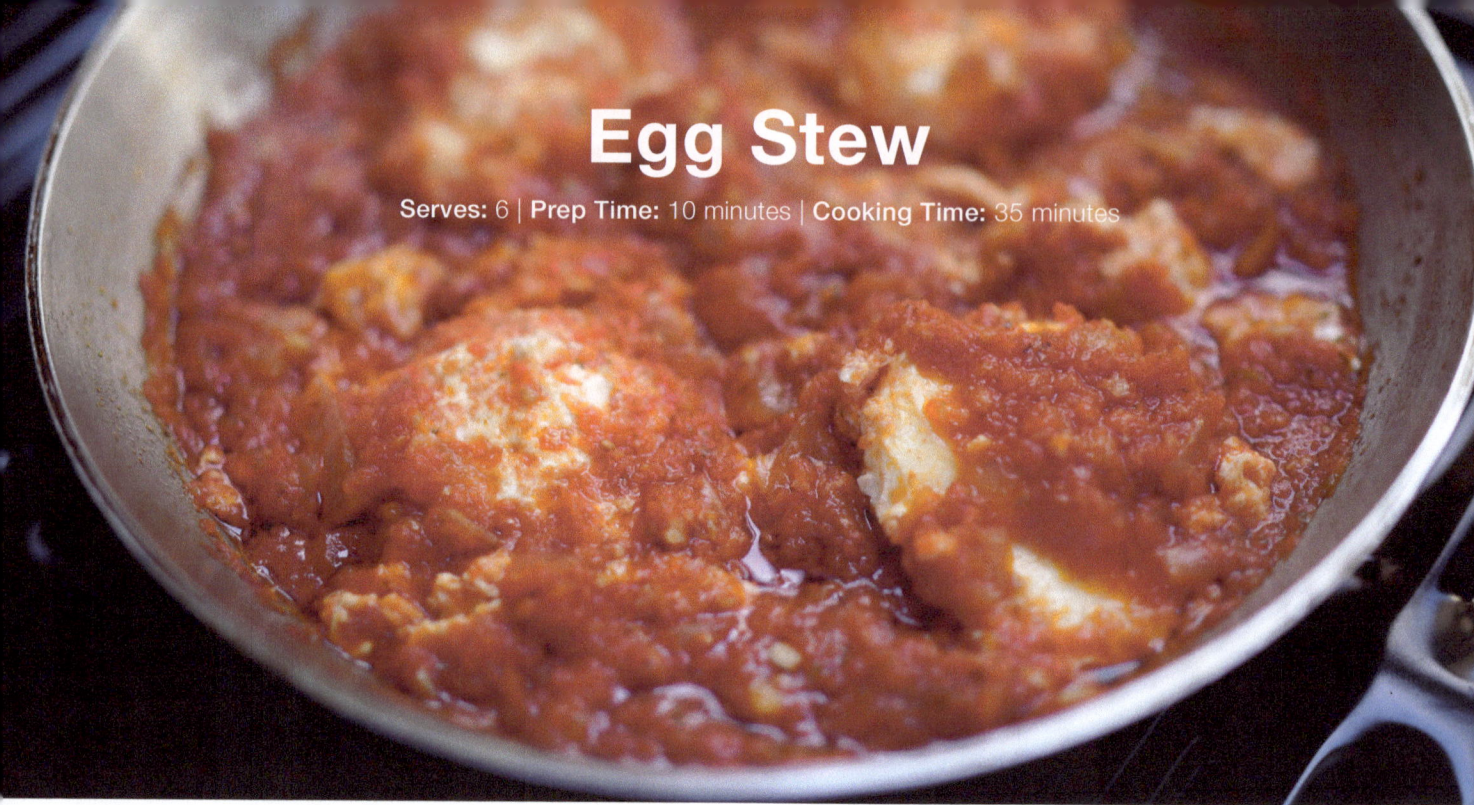

Egg Stew

Serves: 6 | **Prep Time:** 10 minutes | **Cooking Time:** 35 minutes

For Stew

- 8 medium tomatoes (2lbs/1kg)
- 1 large yellow onion (10oz/284g), chopped, onion ring quarters
- 8 Kpakpo Shitɔ (5 Scotch Bonnet/2 Habanero) pepper, finely chopped
- 4 cloves garlic, finely chopped
- 3½ tsp ginger, freshly minced
- 10 tbsp (5fl oz/148ml) vegetable oil
- 1½ tsp salt
- ½ tsp curry powder
- 2 tsp tomato puree (or paste)

For Eggs

- 6 free range eggs

Preparation

1. In a saucepan, combine oil, yellow onion, ginger, garlic, Kapkpo Shitɔ (Scotch Bonnet) and salt over high heat for about 5–7 minutes, stirring continuously.

2. Add tomato puree to sizzling onion mix when onion soften and begin to turn golden brown on the edges. Continue stirring for 2 minutes, mixing in puree.

3. Meanwhile, cut tomatoes into quarters and blend in a food processor or blender.

4. Add blended tomatoes and mix completely. Cover saucepan with lid and let cook.

5. After 10 minutes reduce heat to medium and tip lid slightly to partly cover saucepan to allow some steam to escape. Add curry powder and let stew continue to cook for 5 minutes, stirring occasionally.

6. Reach for the eggs. Crack egg one after the other and gently drop into the stew, making sure to space eggs evenly in the stew. Do not stir. Cover with lid.

7. After 3 minutes flip the eggs. Again, do not stir stew. Cover for 2 more minutes as the eggs cook and each take on its own beautiful individual imperfect circular shape.

8. Reduce heat to low, partly cover with lid and let simmer for 5 more minutes. Turn heat off, the Egg Stew is ready to be consumer with a side or in bread as a sandwich.

> **Tip: Raise the temperature!**
> Reduce or add more Kpakpo Shitɔ (Scotch Bonnet) pepper to increase the pepper heat level to hot or keep it mild.

Gari Foto

Serves: 6
Prep Time: 10 minutes
Cooking Time: 40 minutes

For Stew
- 8 medium tomatoes (2lbs/1kg)
- 1 large yellow onion (10oz/284g), finely chopped
- 5 Kpakpo Shitɔ (3 Scotch Bonnet/1 Habanero) pepper, finely chopped
- 4 cloves garlic, finely chopped
- 2 tsp ginger, freshly minced
- 10 tbsp (5fl oz/148ml) vegetable oil
- 1½ tsp salt
- 2 tsp tomato puree (or paste)

For Gari Mix
- 6 cups (32oz/900g) Gari (pan-roasted Cassava grains)
- 2 cups (16fl oz/474ml) water

For Garnishing
- 1 green bell pepper (green sweet pepper), de-seeded, freshly chopped

Preparation

1. In a saucepan, combine oil, red onion, ginger, garlic, Kpakpo shitɔ and salt over high heat for about 5–7 minutes, stirring continuously.

2. Add tomato puree to sizzling red onion mix when onion bits soften and begin to turn golden brown on the edges. Continue stirring for 2 minutes, mixing in puree.

3. As onion mix sizzles, clean, and cut tomatoes into quarters and blend in a food processor or blender. Add blended tomatoes and mix completely. Cover saucepan with lid and let cook for 10 minutes.

4. Reduce heat to medium and tip lid slightly to partly cover saucepan to allow some steam to escape.

5. Stir occasionally as cooking continues for 15 more minutes, then bring heat to low and let simmer for about 5–10 minutes. Turn stove off.

6. Pour the Gari into a large serving bowl. Gradually add water while stirring with a fork to prevent lumps from forming until enough water is added to get Gari mixture damp.

7. Using a ladle, add stew to Gari mixture and mix with the fork. Add stew, ladle by ladle, until the entire mixture of Gari is generously coated with the stew.

8. Add green pepper, and any veggies of choice and stir into Gari mixture. Serve the Gari Foto as is, or with some fried or grilled fish.

Goat Stew

Serves: 6 | **Prep Time:** 10 minutes | **Cooking Time:** 50 minutes

Goat Stew is a serious delicacy that you cannot and must not be taken lightly. The act of continuous practice of this same goat stew will eventually lead to a good Ghana Goat Jollof Rice that will silence many for years to come.

The obvious thing is to first get the best well-raised goat from your farmer or butcher. A nice cut of fresh goat meat, trimmed of excess fat, is how to start this delicious adventure. Then stretch a bit and get hands-on to start this adventure. Drink loads of water. Haha, just kidding! Maybe turn up your favourite African music playlist to electrify you and get you in the groove to zoom right into action. Happy Goat Stewing!

For Steaming Goat
• 2lbs (32oz/907g) fresh goat, cleaned, trimmed of excess fat, cut to bite-sized chunks
• ½ large red onion, finely chopped
• 6 cloves garlic, finely chopped
• 4 tsp minced ginger
• 1½ tsp salt

For Grilling Goat
• 1 tbsp vegetable oil

For Stew

- 8 medium tomatoes (2lbs/1kg), chopped
- ½ large (5oz/142g) red onion, chopped, onion ring quarters
- 1 large yellow onion (10oz/284g), chopped, onion ring quarters
- 5 Scotch Bonnet (3 Habanero) pepper, finely chopped
- 6 cloves garlic, finely chopped
- 4 tsp ginger, freshly minced
- 2 tsp salt
- 2 tsp tomato puree (or paste)

Preparation

1. Place goat pieces in cooking pot over high heat, add onion, ginger, garlic and salt. Stir occasionally for about 6–8 minutes for onion to start caramelizing and goat browning begins. Cover pot and let steam for about 5 minutes. Turn heat off and uncover. Save any steaming juice and stock leftovers in cooking pot.

2. Preheat grill or turn the broiler of your cooking unit on to medium. Using a fork, place goat pieces in grill pan and toss with 1 tablespoon oil. Let the goat pieces grill for about 20 minutes. Flip at least once halfway for even grilling and all sides.

3. Meanwhile, begin the stew by adding oil, red onion, yellow onion, ginger, garlic, Scotch Bonnet and salt in a large saucepan for about 5–7 minutes over high heat. Stir continuously.

4. Add tomato puree to sizzling mix when onion bits soften and begin to turn golden brown on the edges. Continue stirring for about 2 minutes, mixing in puree.

5. Add chopped tomatoes and mix completely. Cover saucepan with lid and let cook for about 10 minutes. Then reduce heat to medium and tip lid slightly so saucepan is partly covered to allow some steam to escape. Add saved steaming stock and continue cooking, stirring occasionally.

6. After 10 minutes add grilled goat pieces with any residue in grill pan. Reduce heat to medium low and let simmer for about 5–10 minutes. Stir at least once during this time.

7. Turn heat off, replace lid completely on saucepan and let rest for 5 minutes. Grab your plates and enjoy some delicious goat stew.

> **Tip: Raise the temperature or not!**
> Add extra Scotch Bonnet (Habanero) pepper to increase the pepper heat level or reduce the amount to bring the heat level down.

Waakye Stew

Serves: 4 | **Prep Time:** 10 minutes | **Cooking Time:** 55 minutes

For Steaming Beef

- 2lbs (32oz/907g) fresh beef, cleaned, trimmed of excess fat, cut to bite-sized chunks
- 6 cloves garlic, finely chopped
- ½ large red onion, finely chopped
- 1 pod Hwentia (Grains of Selim)
- 1 tsp white or black pepper
- 1½ tsp salt
- 2 tsp minced ginger

For Boiling Wele

- ¾lb (12oz/340g) Wele (preserved cow hide), cleaned
- 2 cups (16fl oz/474ml) water
- 2 tsp salt
- 1 pod Hwentia (Grains of Selim)

For Frying

- 12 tbsp vegetable oil

For Stew

- 8 medium tomatoes (2lbs/1kg), blended
- ½ large (5oz/142g) red onion, finely chopped
- 1 large yellow onion (10oz/284g), finely chopped
- 4 Scotch Bonnet (2 Habanero) pepper, finely chopped
- 2 Akweley Waabii (red finger hot pepper/fresh cayenne), finely chopped
- 8 cloves garlic, finely chopped
- 5 tsp ginger, freshly minced
- ¾ tsp Nkitinkiti (Anise Seed)
- 2 tsp salt
- 2 tsp tomato puree (or paste)
- 2 tsp thyme leaves

Preparation

1. Place beef in cooking pot over high heat and add salt, ginger, garlic, Hwentia, white pepper and red onion bits. Stir occasionally for about 6–8 minutes for onion to start caramelizing and until browns. Cover pot and let steam for about 2–3 minutes. Turn heat off, uncover, and pick out beef onto plate to cool. Save any steaming juice and stock leftovers.

2. Boil Wele with 2 cups water, 1 pod Hwentia (Grains of Selim) and salt over high heat in another cooking pot for about 15 minutes. Drain and discard liquid after.

3. Meanwhile, grab a saucepan, and heat oil over medium heat. Once the oil is hot, fry beef pieces in batches by placing in oil for 3–4 minutes on each side. Flip and repeat. Be careful as oil might splatter. Use a splatter screen for protection. Set fried beef pieces aside on a plate.

4. Begin the stew by adding red onion, yellow onion, ginger, garlic, Scotch Bonnet, Akweley Waabii (fresh cayenne) and salt into the oil for about 5–7 minutes once last batch of beef is out. Stir continuously.

5. Add tomato puree to sizzling red onion mix when onion bits soften and begin to turn golden brown on the edges. Continue stirring for about 2 minutes, mixing in puree.

6. Add chopped tomatoes and mix completely. Cover saucepan with lid and let cook for about 10 minutes. Then reduce heat to medium and tip lid slightly so saucepan is partly covered to allow some steam to escape.

7. Add saved steaming beef stock and continue cooking, stirring occasionally. After 5 minutes add fried beef pieces with any residue oil in the plate. Add Wele, Nkitinkiti (Anise Seed), and thyme leaves. Stir to mix completely. Reduce heat to low and let simmer for about 15 minutes. Stir at least twice during this time.

8. Turn heat off, replace lid completely on saucepan and let rest for about 5 minutes. Grab your plates and enjoy some delicious Waakye stew with Waakye or something else.

> **Tip 1: Raise the temperature or not!**
> Add extra Scotch Bonnet (Habanero) pepper to increase the pepper heat level or reduce the Scotch Bonnet to bring the heat level down.

> **Tip 2: Bake beef instead of frying**
> The beef can be placed in oven at 400°F (200°C/ Gas 6) for 25–30 minutes instead of frying.

> **Tip 3: Steam beef extra 5–10 minutes**
> Let beef continue to steam for an extra 5–10 minutes if not interested in frying. Then carry on with making the stew till you need to add beef and simmer.

> **Tip 4: Chop tomatoes easily!**
> Use a serrated or bread knife to chop tomatoes easily.

GHANA JOLLOF RICE 3.0 & BEYOND

Some people say they cook the best Jollof Rice! But, one can only believe that when they have not had the chance to try true Ghana Jollof Rice.

Jollof Rice, the most popular dish out of West Africa, traces its origin to the Wolof Empire of West Africa, in the region where present-day Gambia and Senegal are located. Senegal's Thieboudienne, made with rice, fish, chunks of vegetables and more, is the ancestor and root of all Jollof Rice. Centuries on, with people migrating, the dish has spread all over West Africa. Over time, the name of the rice from the land of Wolof, or Wolof Rice, eventually morphed into Jollof Rice.

Generations after generations made their own versions of what their families passed on to them before demarcation of countries. Jollof Rice is a one-pot dish of rice, cooked in vegetable stew or with meats. It comes close to a pilau but takes on its own West African character, style, and attitude. Please be advised to not try messing with a person from the Republic of Jollof Rice especially on matters related to Jollof Rice unless you know you can handle the passionate Jollof Rice citizens.

Today, almost every West African country claim its own version of Jollof Rice. Nevertheless, only one Western African country, Ghana, obviously, knows that Jollof Rice is also called Jorley Rice. Jorley Rice is not even known to some younger generations of Ghanaians. The word Jorley, from the Ga language, is a word used to refer to that special person one is in love with and will defy all odds to be with that special person. Jorley is someone you love so much who you will do anything for and fight for that love till the very end to spend life together as a married couple. The word Jorley is not exactly recorded in history as to when it was first used, but dates back to the days before Ghana's independence. It gained more traction after Ghana's independence and with Highlife music.

Jorley Rice, the true Ghana Jollof Rice, is passionately made with heart and soul as a dish for the special person or persons around you that you will go beyond the oceans to show love. This is how deep Ghana Jollof Rice is to Ghanaians.

The concept of a pot of Ghana Jollof Rice is love and not a showing off game. Let your Jollof Rice speak for itself. I bet my "brodas and sistas" in a country near Ghana don't know. The heart, soul, and passion of love are what Ghana Jollof Rice is built on and with little bits of blessing from the land of Ghana. No wonder I was once asked in a cooking class by a lady, "is it true what they say about Jollof Rice that you can get and keep a husband if you know how to cook Jollof?" Listen my people, it's true! Your Jorley will remain as long as you have that Ghana Jollof Rice skill mastered and keep the fresh plate of Ghana Jollof Rice going. Obviously, you must also learn to produce that lightly scorched rusty Ghana Jollof Rice crust at the bottom of the cooking pot – Jollof Shishi or Jollof Asie or Jollof Kanzo. You are disqualified if you burn the rice, and you must hide your face in the event of burning the rice.

The art of attaining a tasty pot of Ghana Jollof Rice is an art form mastered only by practice. Or better still, from apprenticeship under that tutelage of a Ghana Jollof Rice warrior. Remember, my friends, you cannot talk your way to the top. The technique must be studied well and practiced flawlessly in order to attain the skills that turn heads.

Should anyone speak of a superior Jollof Rice to you again, kindly ask them to cook it to support their talk with real evidence. It's the least one can ask. This means you must have really practiced it well to be able to "walk the talk" yourself whenever called upon. Then you can join in and say, as we say in Ghana, "show them where the power lies." Pure and simple: Ghana Jollof Rice. "No libilibi! No labalaba!"(a Ghanaian saying meaning no tricks, nothing hidden, everything in plain sight). Welcome to Ghana Jollof Rice 3.0! The third generation of this pot of love is out and about.

Ghana Jollof Rice

Serves: 8 | **Prep Time:** 15 minutes | **Cooking Time:** 65 minutes

Remember, you must also learn to produce that lightly scorched rusty Ghana Jollof Rice crust at the bottom of the cooking pot – Ghana Jollof Shishi or Ghana Jollof Asie or Ghana Jollof Kanzo. You are disqualified if you burn the rice, and you must hide your face in the event of burning the rice.

For Tomato Stew

- 12 medium tomatoes (3lbs/1.5kg)
- 1 large red onion (10oz/284g), finely chopped
- 1 small yellow onion (4oz/113g), finely chopped
- 8 Kpakpo Shitɔ (Shito), finely chopped
- 3 Scotch Bonnet (2 Habanero) pepper, finely chopped
- 6 cloves garlic, finely chopped
- 2 tbsp ginger root, finely chopped
- 16 tbsp (8fl oz/237ml) vegetable oil
- 2½ tsp salt
- 4 tsp tomato puree (or paste)

For Rice

- 2½lbs (40oz/1.1Kg) long-grain rice
- 3½ cups (28fl oz/840ml) boiling water
- 2½ tsp salt
- ¾ tsp curry powder
- 2 fresh bay leaves
- 1 sprig fresh basil

> **Tip 1: Use a cooking pot with heavy bottom and tight-fitting lid for best results**
> For the best result Ghana Jollof, use cooking pots with heavy bottom to keep the Jollof from easily sticking to the bottom and a tight-fitting lid to fully trap steam.

Preparation

1. In a large cooking pot, combine oil, onions, ginger, garlic, Kpakpo Shitɔ, Scotch Bonnet and salt over high heat for about 7–10 minutes, stirring continuously.

2. Add tomato puree to sizzling red onion mix when onion bits soften and begin to turn golden brown on the edges. Continue stirring for about 2 minutes, mixing in puree.

3. As onion mix sizzles, clean and cut tomatoes into quarters and blend in a food processor or blender.

4. Add blended tomatoes and mix completely. Cover cooking pot with lid and let cook.

5. After 10 minutes reduce heat to medium and tip lid slightly so cooking pot is partly covered to allow some steam to escape. Let stew cook for 20 minutes, stirring occasionally.

6. Wash rice and add to boiling stew. Stir continuously until rice absorbs the stew. Stirring also helps prevent rice from sticking to bottom of the pot.

7. Add boiling water, salt, curry powder and increase heat to medium-high. Mix completely and let boil.

8. Continue stirring till the rice absorbs almost all the liquid. Add bay leaf and cover pot with lid. Reduce heat to the lowest temperature. Let rice cook for about 20–25 minutes. Use fork to stir and turn rice at least once, half way into cooking (around the 10–12 minutes mark). Add basil during this time.

9. Turn heat off and let stand for about 5 minutes without opening pot. Jollof Rice is ready to be served as is or with a side of vegetables, salads and meats of your choice.

> **Tip 2: Oven Ghana Jollof Rice**
> A tasty Ghana Jollof Rice requires steam. Once the rice absorbs the stew, it can be transferred into a large glass baking dish. Tightly wrap bakeware top with foil and bake in oven at 400°F (200°C/ Gas 6) for 10 minutes longer than required duration.

> **Tip 3: Raise the temperature or not!**
> Add extra Scotch Bonnet (Habanero) pepper to increase the pepper heat level or reduce the Scotch Bonnet to bring the heat level down.

Brown Rice Ghana Jollof Rice

We raised the stakes a little and went brown rice. Who knew? Brown Rice Ghana Jollof Rice adds a new Jollof Rice category and puts that smoky Ghana flavour into it.

For Tomato Stew

- 12 medium tomatoes (3lbs/1.5kg)
- 1 large red onion (10oz/284g), finely chopped
- 1 small yellow onion (4oz/113g), finely chopped
- 8 Kpakpo Shitɔ (Shito), finely chopped
- 3 Scotch Bonnet (2 Habanero) pepper, finely chopped
- 6 cloves garlic, finely chopped
- 2 tbsp ginger root, finely chopped
- 16 tbsp (8fl oz/237ml) vegetable oil
- 2½ tsp salt
- 4 tsp tomato puree (or paste)

For Brown Rice

- 2¼lbs (36oz/1Kg) jasmine brown rice
- 4¼ cups (34fl oz/1L) boiling water
- 2 tsp salt
- ¾ tsp curry powder
- 2 fresh bay leaves
- 1 sprig fresh basil

For Smoked Fish

- 1lb (16oz/½kg) smoked mackerel or tuna

Preparation

1. In a large cooking pot, combine oil, onions, ginger, garlic, Kpakpo Shito, Scotch Bonnet and salt over high heat for about 7–10 minutes, stirring continuously.

2. Add tomato puree to sizzling red onion mix when onion bits soften and begin to turn golden brown on the edges. Continue stirring for about 2 minutes, mixing in puree.

3. As onion mix sizzles, clean, and cut tomatoes into quarters and blend in a food processor or blender.

4. Add blended tomatoes and mix completely. Cover cooking pot with lid and let cook.

5. After 10 minutes reduce heat to medium and tip lid slightly so cooking pot is partly covered to allow some steam to escape. Let stew cook for 15 minutes, stirring occasionally.

6. Meanwhile, remove skin of smoked mackerel or tuna and break into bite-size pieces. Add and mix thoroughly into stew. Continue cooking for 5 minutes.

7. Wash jasmine brown rice and add to boiling stew. Stir continuously until rice absorbs the stew. Stirring also helps prevent rice from sticking to bottom of the pot.

8. Add boiling water, salt, curry powder and increase heat to medium-high. Mix completely and let boil.

9. Continue stirring till the rice absorbs almost all the liquid. Add bay leaf and cover pot with lid. Reduce heat to the lowest temperature. Let rice cook for about 30 minutes. Use fork to stir and turn rice at least once, halfway into cooking (around the 15 minutes mark). Add basil during this time.

10. Turn stove off and let stand for about 10 minutes without opening pot. The Brown Rice Ghana Jollof Rice is ready to be served as is or with a side of vegetables, salads and meats of your choice.

Tip 1: Go without smoked fish
The smoked fish can be omitted from the Brown Rice Ghana Jollof Rice.

Tip 2: Raise the temperature
Add extra Scotch Bonnet (Habanero) pepper to increase the pepper heat level or reduce the Scotch Bonnet to bring the heat level down.

Tip 3: Use a cooking pot with heavy bottom
For the best result, use a cooking pot with heavy bottom to keep the Jollof from easily sticking to the bottom and a tight-fitting lid to fully trap steam.

Ghana Goat Jollof Rice

Serves: 8 | Prep Time: 20 minutes | Cooking Time: 75 minutes

For Steaming Goat

- 2lbs (32oz/907g) fresh goat, cleaned, trimmed of excess fat, cut to bite-sized chunks
- ½ large red onion, finely chopped
- 6 cloves garlic, finely chopped
- 4 tsp minced ginger
- 1½ tsp salt

For Rice

- 2½lbs (40oz/1.1Kg) long-grain rice
- 3½ cups (28fl oz/840ml) boiling water
- 2½ tsp salt
- 1 tsp curry powder
- 2 fresh bay leaves
- 1 sprig fresh basil

For Grilling Goat

- 1 tbsp vegetable oil

For Tomato Stew

- 12 medium tomatoes (3lbs/1.5kg)
- 1 large red onion (10oz/284g), chopped, onion ring quarters
- 1 large yellow onion (10oz/284g), chopped, onion ring quarters
- 8 Kpakpo Shito (Shito), finely chopped
- 3 Scotch Bonnet (2 Habanero) pepper, finely chopped
- 8 cloves garlic, finely chopped
- 2 tbsp ginger root, finely chopped
- 16 tbsp (8fl oz/237ml) vegetable oil
- 2½ tsp salt
- 4 tsp tomato puree (or paste)

Preparation

1. Place goat pieces in cooking pot over high heat and add onion, ginger, garlic, and salt. Stir occasionally for about 6–8 minutes for onion to start caramelizing and goat browning begins. Cover pot and let steam for about 5 minutes. Turn heat off and uncover. Save any steaming juice and stock leftovers in cooking pot.

2. Preheat grill or turn the broiler of your cooking unit on to medium. Using a fork, place goat pieces in grill pan and toss with 1 tablespoon oil. Let the goat pieces grill for about 20 minutes. Flip at least once halfway for even grilling and all sides.

3. Meanwhile, begin the stew by adding oil, red onion, yellow onion, ginger, garlic, Kpakpo Shito, Scotch Bonnet and salt in a large saucepan for about 5–7 minutes over high heat. Stir continuously.

4. Add tomato puree to sizzling mix when onion bits soften and begin to turn golden brown on the edges. Continue stirring for about 2 minutes, mixing in puree.

5. Add chopped tomatoes and mix completely. Cover saucepan with lid and let cook for about 10 minutes. Then reduce heat to medium and tip lid slightly so saucepan is partly covered to allow some steam to escape. Add saved steaming stock and continue cooking, stirring occasionally.

6. After 10 minutes add grilled goat pieces with any residue in grill pan. Mix thoroughly and let stew continue to cook over medium heat.

7. After 10 minutes, wash rice and add to boiling stew. Stir until rice absorbs the stew. Stirring also helps prevent rice from sticking to the bottom of the pot.

8. Add boiling water, salt, curry powder and increase heat to medium-high. Mix completely and let boil.

9. Continue stirring till the rice absorbs almost all the liquid. Add bay leaf and cover pot with lid. Reduce heat to the lowest temperature. Let rice cook for about 20–25 minutes. Use fork to stir and turn rice at least once, halfway into cooking (around 10–12 minutes mark). Add basil during this time.

10. Turn heat off and let rest for about 5 minutes without opening pot. The pot of Goat Jollof Rice is ready to be served with a side of vegetables, salads and other side choices.

Tip 1: Raise the temperature or not!
Add extra Scotch Bonnet (Habanero) pepper to increase the pepper heat level or reduce the Scotch Bonnet to bring the heat level down.

Tip 2: Use a cooking pot with heavy bottom
For the best result Ghana Jollof, use a cooking pot with heavy bottom to keep the Jollof from easily sticking to the bottom and a tight-fitting lid to fully trap steam.

Tip 3: Steam goat extra 5 minutes
Let goat continue to steam for an extra 5 minutes if not into grilling. Then carry on with making stew till you need to add goat and simmer.

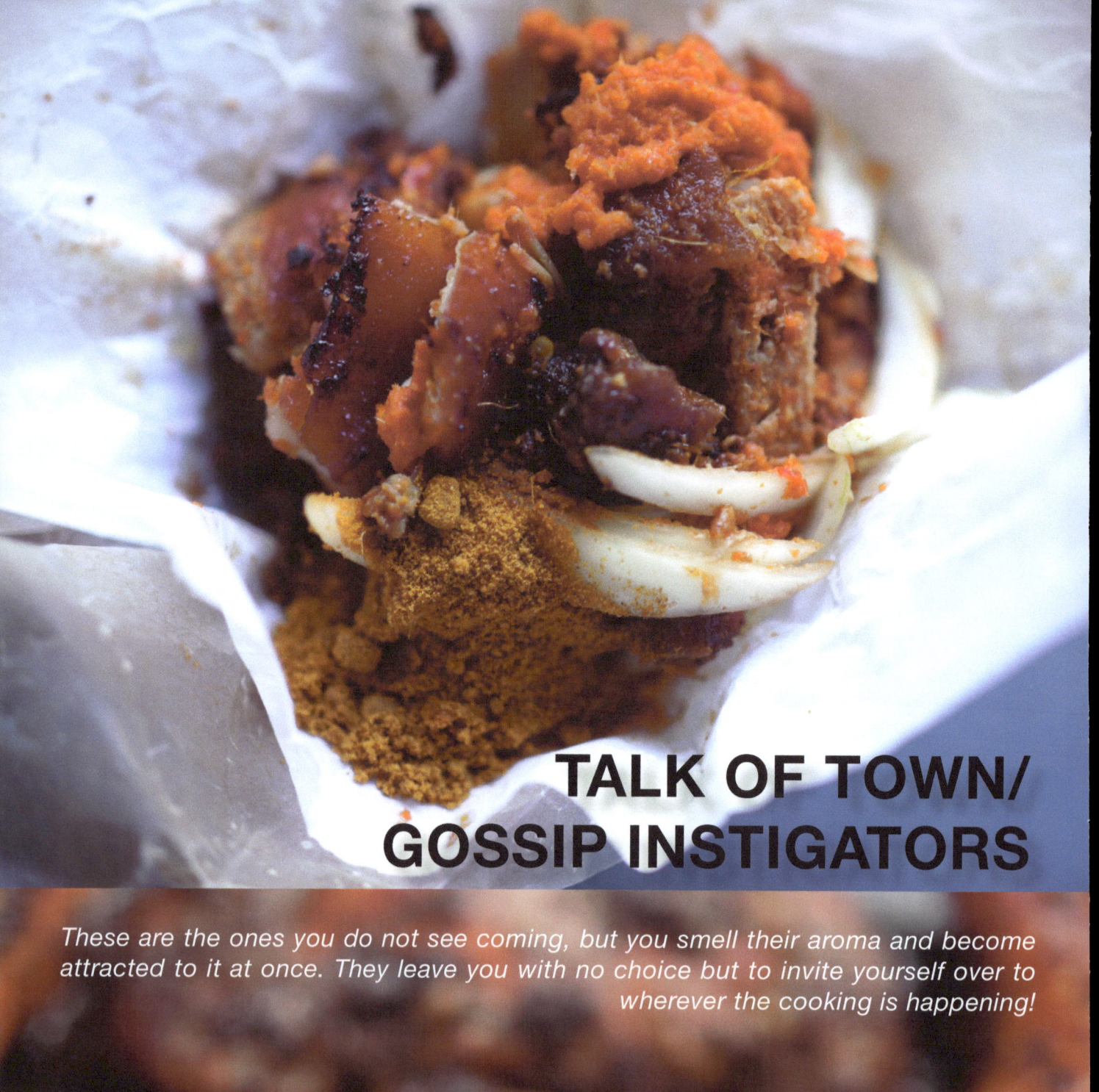

TALK OF TOWN/ GOSSIP INSTIGATORS

These are the ones you do not see coming, but you smell their aroma and become attracted to it at once. They leave you with no choice but to invite yourself over to wherever the cooking is happening!

Grouper Khebab

Serves: 6
Prep Time: 15 minutes
Khebab Time: 25 minutes

A fish lovers khebab for any day of no heavy lifting.

For Grouper

• 1 large Grouper (5 lbs/80oz/2½kg), scaled, gutted, cleaned, fillet
• 5 tsp ginger, freshly minced
• 2 tsp white or black pepper
• 3¼ tsp salt
• 6 tbsp flour

For Frying Grouper

• 12 tbsp (6fl oz/177ml) vegetable oil

For Green Bell Pepper

• 1 green bell pepper (green sweet pepper), de-seeded, freshly into squares

For Skewer Veg Quick Stir-Fry

• 2 medium cucumbers, washed, cut into quarters lengthwise, chopped, ½-inch (12mm) in thickness
• 2 medium red onion (8oz/227g), peeled, cut into quarters, roots trimmed at bottom
• 3 carrots, washed, peeled, ¼-inch (6mm) thick round slices
• 2 tbsp vegetable oil
• 1 tsp salt

For Skewers

• 12 bamboo skewers

Preparation

1. Cut Grouper into about 2-inch by 1-inch rectangles. Place in a bowl, spice with ginger, white pepper and salt. Cover and let marinade for 10 minutes.

2. Meanwhile combine cucumber pieces, carrot coins and red onions pieces with 2 tablespoon vegetable oil in a pan over high heat for quick stir-fry. Stir continuously for 5 minutes. Turn heat off and let cool, do not cover.

3. Grab a frying pan, and heat oil over medium heat to fry fish. Dust Grouper rectangles lightly with flour on all sides.

4. Fry fish in batches by placing in oil for 1–3 minutes on each side, until golden brown. Flip and repeat. Be careful as oil may splatter. Use a splatter screen for protection. Set fried fish aside on paper lined plate.

5. Thread fried Grouper rectangle gently onto the skewers, 3 or 4 fried fish rectangles on each skewer and alternate with cucumber, carrot ring, onion pieces and green bell pepper square. Each skewer will be fried fish, cucumber, carrot, onion, green bell pepper then fried fish, cucumber, carrot, onion, green bell pepper, and repeat in that order until all fried fish rectangles are used.

6. There you have it. Grouper Khebab is ready to put smiles on faces.

> **Tip: Add some red**
> Use red bell peppers (red sweet pepper) to add some more popping red colour.

Blema Turkey Kpakpa

Serves: 5 | Prep Time: 15 minutes | Roasting Time: 95 minutes

In honour of the late K.T. Glover, a man who never played with his turkey.

This recipe is in honour of my late grandfather. He was so present in my life growing up, not only with his physical presence, but also because of his stories as a soldier in World War II, knowledge of world history, travel experience, and activities as head of the family. He had an open and loving heart to see the best in everyone. During his travels, he never returned without a turkey. The only exemption was that the place he visited did not have turkeys or it was probably not worth going through the trouble to carry it along.

Blema Turkey Kpakpa, meaning Good Old-Fashioned Turkey or Good Old School Turkey, is a salute to my late grandfather and pays homage to his contemporaries. "Tsutsu blema," was the popular beginning words that my late grandparents, grandaunts, granduncles, and older folks used to introduce historical events and start stories told during my childhood. Most of these stories predated Ghana's independence and were very colourful depictions of people and places as well as events and occurrences that molded and shaped them. This is one attempt to keep a little part of the old story tradition going with this delicious turkey recipe. Enjoy!

For Turkey

• 5 lbs (80oz/2½kg) turkey thigh, cleaned, trimmed of excess fat

• 2 ½ tsp salt

• 3 tbsp olive oil

For Blema Spice

• 4oz (113g) ginger root, peeled

• 3 sprigs fresh basil

• 4 cloves garlic

• 2 spring onions (scallions)

• 5 tbsp crush red pepper

• 10 tbsp water

Preparation

1. Preheat oven to 450°F (230°C/ Gas 8).

2. Combine ginger, basil, garlic, white part of spring onions (scallions), crushed red pepper and 7 tablespoons water in a blender. Blitz into a paste. Rinse blender with remaining water and mix into the paste.

3. Place turkey in a glass roasting pan or heavy-duty roasting pan of choice. Salt the pieces and use the spice to generously coat every piece. Save any remaining spice.

4. Drizzle with olive oil and place in oven to roast. After 10 minutes, reduce heat to 400°F (200°C/ Gas 6). Let continue roasting for about 30 minutes.

5. Reduce heat to 375°F (190°C/Gas 5). Continue to roast for 55 more minutes.

6. Halfway into entire roasting time, baste turkey pieces with juice from bottom of roasting pan. Baste at least once before the entire roasting time is completed.

7. Turn off heat and let rest for 10 minutes. Garnish with finely chopped green leaf part of the spring onions (scallions) and serve with sides of your choice.

Tip 1: Marinade turkey overnight
Generously coat turkey with Blema spice, cover and let marinade overnight in refrigerator.

Tip 2: Whole turkey roast
When roasting a whole turkey, let roast an extra 25–40 minutes at 350°F (180°C/ Gas 8) depending on size of turkey. Also, double the ingredients for the spice.

1-2-3 Ghana Pepper Chicken

Serves: 5 | Prep Time: 10 minutes | Roasting Time: 35 minutes

Let your hair strands stand up for a minute and clear your sinus for some sweet sweat. It's tasty with some heat and sweetness. If you don't know pepper, don't try this; you might sweat. Try with Akonfem (Guinea Fowl) and other poultry, too. Cheers!

For Chicken

- 4lbs chicken breast, cleaned, trimmed of excess fat
- 2 tsp salt
- 3 tbsp olive oil

For 1-2-3 Spice

- 4oz (113g) ginger root, peeled
- a handful of Kpakpo Shitɔ (Pettie Belle Pepper)
- 10 Scotch Bonnet (6 Habanero)
- 6 Akweley Waabii (red finger hot pepper/fresh cayenne)
- 6 tbsp water

Tip 1: Marinade overnight
Generously coat chicken with spice, and marinade overnight.

Tip 2: Whole chicken roast or try with Guinea Fowl or other poultry.
Roast an extra 15–20 minutes at 350°F (180°C/ Gas 8) for whole a chicken, depending on size and double the ingredients for the spice. Try the spice on a whole Akonfem (Guinea Fowl) or any other poultry of choice.

Preparation

1. Preheat oven to 450°F (230°C/ Gas 8).

2. Combine ginger and peppers with 4 tablespoons water in a blender. Blitz into a paste. Rinse blender with remaining water and mix into the paste.

3. Place chicken breast in a glass roasting pan or heavy-duty roasting pan of choice. Salt the pieces and use the spice to generously coat every piece. Save any remaining spice.

4. Drizzle with olive oil and place in oven to roast. After 10 minutes, reduce heat to 400°F (200°C/ Gas 6). Let continue roasting for about 20 minutes.

5. Reduce heat to 350°F (180°C/ Gas 4). Continue to roast for 5-10 more minutes.

6. Halfway into entire roasting time, baste turkey pieces with juice from bottom of roasting pan. Baste at least once before the entire roasting time is completed.

7. Turn off heat, let rest for 10 minutes. Garnish with finely chopped green leaf part of the spring onions (scallions) and serve with sides of your choice.

Chinchinga/Ghana Khebab/Suya

Serves: 6 | Prep Time: 10 minutes | Grilling Time: 25 minutes

For Meat Marinade
- 2 lbs (32oz/1kg) beef sirloin, cleaned
- 1 tbsp minced ginger
- 3 tbsp white vinegar

For Grilling
- 12 wooden or bamboo skewers
- 1 large yellow onion (10oz/284g)
- 4 tbsp vegetable oil

For Chinchinga Spice
- 5½ tbsp cayenne pepper
- 7 tbsp dry roasted groundnut (peanut) powder
- 3 tbsp roasted corn flour
- 3 pods Grains of Selim (guinea pepper), crushed in mortar and pestle or 1 tsp peppercorn
- 1½ tsp salt

Preparation

1. Soak wooden skewers in bowl of water for 15 minutes. Soaking helps keep skewers from burning when grilling.

2. Cut beef into about 2-inch by 1-inch rectangles. Place in a bowl with lid. Mix marinade ingredients together and pour over beef. Mix thoroughly, cover bowl and let marinade for 10 minutes or longer.

3. Mix Chinchinga spice ingredients together in a bowl with spoon.

4. Get the charcoal grill going or preheat grill to medium heat.

5. Remove skewers from water and shake off excess water. Cut onion into quarters and trim the root at bottom of each quarter to let onion layers loose into single pieces.

6. Thread the beef onto the skewers, 3 to 4 beef pieces on each skewer and alternate with onion pieces. Each skewer will be beef, onion, beef, onion, beef etcetera in that order. Repeat until all beef is used.

7. Generously coat each skewer of beef with the Chinchinga spice. Save remaining spice. Drizzle the kebabs with about two tablespoons of oil and place on the grill for about 10–15 minutes, brushing with remaining oil every now and again. Turn and rotated the skewers every so often until brown on all sides and cooked.

8. Remove from grill. Dust with more Chinchinga spice and serve these delicious pieces of meat on a stick.

> **Tip 1: Get some goat**
> Use goat meat instead of beef to bring that goat on deck. Lamb or mutton is always an option too.

> **Tip 2: Go next level with liver**
> Beef liver is a way to take your Chinchinga to the Liver Chinchinga level.

Domɛdo/Clay Oven Baked Pork

Serves: 8 | Prep Time: 10 minutes | Baking Time: 75 minutes

In honour of the late Felix B. Brenya, who knew the full cycle of the pork life very well.

Domɛdo is pronounced "doh-merh-doh." If you know about boxing and you research about boxing in Ghana, one name Azumah Nelson will definitely come up. And if you know the name Azumah Nelson, then you know it was when Ghana reigned in world boxing. The home of Ghana's boxing is a coastal settlement called Bukom, in the capital, Accra. Long before Bukom produced world boxing champs, it also churned a culinary delight known as Domɛdo – a spicy, tasty, baked pork that is baked in a traditional clay oven called "flɔnɔɔ (flornor)" powered with firewood. Domɛdo found its place on Ghana's food map. As oral history has it, Bukom is where Domɛdo originated and started taking root, but Osu became widely known for this street food.

The famous Osu Night Market is a special place in Accra, Ghana, that added to the push of this delicacy. Other nearby coastal communities between these settlements also know the technique of making this dish that is passed on from generation to generation in Ga families of the Ga-Adangbe community in Accra. The combination of spices and right temperature in the traditional clay ovens (Swish Ovens) bake and help melt the fats in an "earth-with-wood" infused atmosphere. The end product is nothing but pure joy of nature for this one-of-a-kind baked pork. And the beauty of this clay oven baking is superb such that the meat takes a golden reddish hue and evenly bakes. Domɛdo is eaten as is or can be eaten with a side of Banku, Kenkey, or Ga Abolo. Others toss chopped Domɛdo into bread, add Domɛdo spice, and sandwich it down with a drink.

For Pork
- 5 lbs (80oz/2½kg) fresh pork, cleaned, cut to 2 chunks
- 3¼ tsp salt

For Domeido Spice
- 8 Akweley Waabii (red finger hot pepper/fresh cayenne)
- ¾ red bell pepper (red sweet pepper), de-seeded
- 1 small (4oz/113g) yellow onion
- 5oz (142g) ginger root, peeled
- 6 cloves garlic
- 6 tbsp water
- 2 tbsp cayenne pepper

Preparation
1. Preheat oven to 450°F (230°C/Gas 8).

2. Combine ginger root, garlic yellow onion, red bell pepper and red finger hot pepper and 4 tablespoons water in a blender. Blitz into a paste. Rinse blender with remaining water and mix into the paste. Add cayenne pepper and mix.

3. Place pork in heavy-duty oven pan. Salt the pieces and use the spice to generously coat each piece. Save any remaining spice.

4. Place in oven to bake. After 10 minutes, reduce heat to 375°F (190°C/Gas 5) Let continue baking for about 65 minutes.

5. Reduce heat to 350°F (180°C/Gas 4). Continue to roast for 15 more minutes.

6. Halfway into entire roasting time, baste pork pieces with juice from bottom of roasting pan. Baste at least once before the entire roasting time is completed.

7. Turn off heat, let rest for 10 minutes. Serve Domeido with sides of your choice.

> **Tip 1: Let pork marinade**
> overnight or two nights prior Generously coat pork with Domeido spice and let marinade overnight in refrigerator.

> **Tip 2: Larger size pork**
> For larger size pork, double spice ingredients and bake an extra 15–20 minutes at 350°F (180°C/ Gas 8) for every extra kilogram.

SEE YOU IN GH!

Yooyi
Velvet Tamarind

Whenever the window of opportunity opens and you find yourself in Ghana, try some of these delicious, natural gifts. If you are not sure, ask your host or a local for a second opinion and enjoy your time in tropical Ghana.

Aluguntugui
Sour Sop

Ghana Pineapples

Alasa
African Star Apple

Fresh Cocoa

★ ═══════════════════════════ # INDEX

ABOUT THE AUTHOR

Born and raised in Ghana, history has it that Charles A. Cann made his kitchen debut very early on in life. For the first two decades, Charles was immersed in fresh ingredients, spices, food crops, fruit trees, animals, cooking, baking, and event catering for parties, weddings, and special occasions. Charles never imagined life around the kitchen and food activities would continue into his adulthood.

Years later when Charles found himself at Northwestern University in Evanston, Illinois, he responded to one man's request of helping cook Ghana Jollof Rice for a small gathering. Little did he know that would set the ball in motion and start a whole new food chapter in his life. From that point on, there was one request after another for a prepared dish or a time slot for teaching a recipe. With a full school load and overwhelmed by the requests, Charles created a self-help food recipe online resource.

In 2006, the online resource morphed into the Tropical Ghana Cooking Project in New York City. Charles published his first cookbook, *Tropical Ghana Delights, in 2007*. With the cookbook release, a whole new following gradually grew around Charles' Tropical Ghana cooking, and continues to grow with his classes and workshops. Charles has been featured in *The New York Times Magazine*, *America's Test Kitchen*, *Voice of America*, *Ventures Africa*, and often is called upon for his knowledge of Ghanaian cooking.

Tropical Ghana Kitchen Date is Charles' sophomore cookbook, with a mission to help bring the closest people around anyone even closer with cooking, and those who are far nearer with freshly cooked meals. He also hopes families, friends, and their loved ones can wake up every morning and know that they have more options to eat nutritious and wholesome meals within their kitchen budgets.

In addition to his love of cooking, Charles is also a TV and film professional of more than 20 years. He attended Achimota School, and earned degrees from Harper College, Northwestern University, and Metropolitan College of New York. In 2012, Charles was inducted into the Harper College Distinguished Alumni Class in recognition of his career and service to his community.

www.ingramcontent.com/pod-product-compliance
Lightning Source LLC
Chambersburg PA
CBHW041547120626
46551CB00002B/144